—THE NEW—
FRED WICHE
LAWN & GARDEN
ALMANAC

D1611696

Contents

The New Fred Wiche Lawn & Garden Almanac

Compiled by Bob Hill

Design and production
by Moonlight Graphic Works / Stephen & Debbie Sebree

Edited by Jena Monahan

Assistants on the book:
Jenny Wiche & Janet Hill

Published by
Green Thumb Publishing, Inc.
P.O. Box 3703
Louisville, Kentucky 40201

Printed by Merrick Printing Company, Inc.

ISBN 0-9621352-6-7

Welcome to "The New Fred Wiche Lawn & Garden Almanac." I am especially happy with this book because it includes detailed, month-by-month tips and information on lawn care. It covers mowing, fertilization and pest, disease and weed control. It explains how to plant a new lawn or renovate an old one. It has a section on how to deal with lawn and garden "critters," including moles.

Each monthly chapter begins with a section on lawn care relating to that month. Because weather varies – no two years are ever the same – you might also want to glance at next or last month to see what you should be doing.

The new book also includes chapters on indoor and outdoor organic gardening. It lists the best flowers for hot, dry conditions, tells how to deal with Japanese beetles, how to look for dogwood anthracnose and which vegetables are most susceptible to an early frost. We also kept all the information from our original almanac, with each month divided roughly into three 10-day sections of complete gardening advice.

I would especially like to thank Dr. A.J. Powell Jr., University of Kentucky turf extension specialist, whose new approach to lawn care has caused a lot of us to rethink old methods. I'd also like to thank Donna Michael of the Jefferson County Extension Office, a good friend and excellent horticulturist who, along with extension agents across the Midwest, has kept us better informed on the hobby we most love – gardening.

And, finally, one personal note. Over the years people who have seen our western Shelby County farm have asked, "How do you do all you do and maintain such lovely and productive gardens?"

The answer is simple. Her name is Jenny, my wife and my partner. Our work together is truly a labor of love.

Please enjoy our book.

Fred Wiche
The Weekend Gardener

January

January Checklist

LAWN TIPS

❑ Get the lawn mower tuned up and the blades sharpened.

❑ Get a soil sample to be tested.

EARLY

❑ Turn Christmas tree into a bird feeder.

❑ Plant living Christmas trees.

❑ Continue watering evergreens.

❑ Decide whether to keep Christmas plants or discard them.

❑ Water and fertilize poinsettias and Christmas cactuses.

❑ Check trees for rodent damage.

MIDDLE

❑ Force early flowering trees and shrubs to bloom indoors.

❑ Draw detailed maps of what you would like to do to lawn and garden area.

❑ Check stored bulbs for rot.

❑ Increase humidity around houseplants.

❑ Bring spring-flowering bulbs out of cold storage for blooming indoors.

LATE

❑ Check plants for damage done by salt.

❑ Repot root-bound asparagus fern and other ferns.

SUPER TIP

❑ Raising healthy houseplants.

January may be a slow month for gardening, but it's a great time to begin taking basketball seriously, and that will cover a lot of ground.

January is named for the Roman god Janus, a deity who was pictured with two heads and was thus able to see into the past and the future. It also made him the perfect guy to usher in the new year.

The average high temperature in January in Kentuckiana is 40.8 degrees. The average low is 24.1 degrees. The average precipitation is 3.38 inches, much of it white. That's because "melted snowfall" is also included in precipitation totals — with 10 inches of snow roughly equal to one inch of rain. The average snowfall for January, by the way, is 5.2 inches.

The most precipitation ever to fall on Louisville in January came in 1937, when an astounding 19.17 inches — all of it rain — dropped in. That has since been called, with some reverence, the '37 Flood.

The least precipitation ever to fall in the month was .45 inches, which occurred in 1981. The worst snowstorm in Louisville history dropped 15.7 inches on the city on Jan. 16 and 17 during the awful winter of 1978.

The warmest January day in history occurred in 1943, when the temperature rose to 79 degrees on Jan. 24. The coldest day in the Louisville area was, oddly enough, exactly 20 years later when the temperature on Jan. 24, 1963, dropped to 20 degrees below zero. The thermometer also hit minus 20 in 1884, but who can remember that?

The coldest day in Kentucky history was Jan. 28, 1963, when the temperature dropped to 34 degrees below zero in Cynthiana and Bonnieville.

There are nine hours and 34 minutes of sunlight on Jan. 1, which increases to 10 hours and 15 minutes by Jan. 31. Average soil temperatures — taken at a depth of four inches below a sod cover — range from 33 to 40 degrees.

The late, great Millard Fillmore, who for a president would have made a great gardener, was born Jan. 7, 1800.

LAWN TIPS

So OK, it's January. Your lawn is still in deep hibernation, your lawn mower is shivering in the garage, the Super Bowl still looms ahead, and we want to deliver a brief treatise on the history of lawns — and lawn mowing.

Well, why not? It's always best to know a little about your adversaries before you launch into battle.

According to the folks at the Better Lawn & Turf Institute in Pleasant Hill, Tenn., there are about 50,000 square miles of lawns in the United States, an area larger than Pennsylvania — and we hope not all as hilly.

Broken down, that's more than 53 million households, people who spent almost $6 billion on lawn-care equipment and products, not counting the time invested turning left in the front yard.

In the beginning, of course, this all occurred via orders of a Higher Authority, as told in the Bible: "And God said, let the earth bring forth grass. . . . And the earth brought forth grass. . . ." (Genesis 1:11-12).

As long as 20 million years ago what is now our Great Plains was covered with the grass that had grown there, providing food for all the creatures that roamed the area.

Early Romans were sure to have sheep grazing the lands around their villas so they could see who was coming. In medieval times, from A.D. 500 to the 1400s, lawn areas and turf benches were created for convents, monasteries and the king's palaces as areas of rest, beauty and recreation.

In the early history of this country, the Plains Indians used the thick, tough buffalo grass as sod strips over the framework poles of their houses, a practice continued by the prairie pioneers with sod homes.

Our early settlers along the East Coast, tired of having people looking over their shoulders, first developed the "open yard" or "homestead meadow," so they could also keep a lookout for intruders. It was a landscape very different from the walls and thick hedges common to the European homes they had left behind.

By the 18th century it was very common here in the Colonies to have closely cropped lawns around homes, and the first lawn mower salesman wasn't too far behind. After the first of what we would now call suburbs

sprang up around the great cities of New York and Boston in the early 1800s — houses set back at least 30 feet from the road with tree-lined walks and the first true "front yards"— Saturday mornings would never be the same.

Author and landscaper Frank J. Scott wrote that with these front yards came the sense that its lawn would be "your home's velvet robe." How your lawn looked became very important — not only to you, but to your neighbors.

In the 1920s suburban lawns and gardens were packaged along with pre-fabricated houses and sold by the unit by mail-order houses. After World War II millions of GIs came home to get married, raise families and move to the suburban Levittowns of America — power mowers and lawn sprinklers to follow.

In 1910 about 23 percent of all Americans lived in the suburbs. By 1980 about 60 percent of us lived in the suburbs, and almost 50 million of us were in single-family homes surrounded by lawns.

All this didn't happen without some trials, tribulations and trauma. For the most part, buffalo grass just wouldn't do in the suburbs; grass like that was too tough and not particularly attractive.

Good grass seed was hard to find, especially in a country where the climates ranged from the deep freezes of northern Minnesota to the sauna baths of South Florida.

In the early 1930s the agricultural seed companies saw the developing market in lawn grasses and began selling seed. They did this mainly by just stripping the millions of pounds of common seed from Midwestern fields and selling it. In the 1950s and '60s the seed companies began to spend millions of dollars building better lawn grasses, grasses more specific to certain areas and climates.

Most of the major lawn grasses we have today actually began in this country as immigrants. Seed from European grasses brought here for hay liked the New World so well it spread like prairie fire — especially as the trees were cut down. Alas, some of our worst weeds — crab grass being the worst — arrived here the same way.

Most blue-blooded Kentuckians will be shocked to learn that bluegrass was known back as far as ancient Greece and was actually a familiar meadow grass in northern Europe and England.

It may have been planted in the American Colonies as early as 1586, making its way into Kentucky — and other Midwestern states — with the French explorers. It spread like crazy, only to be "discovered" again when the Daniel Boone-era settlers came through the Cumberland Gap.

No matter how it got here, it did very well in Kentucky, and as better varieties were developed the fame of the Kentucky Bluegrass spread with them.

The care and feeding practices for maintaining a good lawn have evolved nearly as much as the grasses themselves. In the really good old days, sheep, cattle and even rabbits — can you imagine a few hundred well-trained rabbits hopping about on a suburban lawn of today? — were used to maintain the lawn. For the bigger projects, the kings and queens could also dispatch a few hundred serfs armed with scythes.

That changed in 1783 when a man named Edwin Budding, a textile engineer from Gloucestershire, England, received a patent on the lawn mower, a patent accompanied with the biggest lie in history.

This application, he said, will provide "an amusing, useful and healthful exercise."

What Budding had devised was the "reel" lawn mower — an idea taken from the spiral cutting mechanism used to shear napped fabrics in textile mills. By 1852 an English company had marketed 1,500 of these newfangled devices — some models to be pulled by a horse, a donkey or two men.

In 1902 another Englishman, James Edward Ransome, built the first motor-driven lawn mower. Not be be outdone, an American, Col. Edward George, attached a gasoline engine from his washing machine to his hand mower and soon began manufacturing "Moto-Mowers."

Rotary mowers were first developed in the 1930s, followed by home riding mowers, weed-eaters and electric edgers, followed by — history does move in circles — the rise in lawn-care companies that dispatch a few hundred employees to service your lawn for you.

But we do remain a do-it-ourselves country. In 1990 Americans bought 6.8 million lawn mowers, including 1.1 million riding mowers, a decided improvement over well-trained rabbits.

LAWN THINGS TO DO IN JANUARY:
Get the lawn mower tuned up and the
blades sharpened.
Unless a pickax is required, get a soil
sample to be tested.

GARDEN TIPS
EARLY

Yes, it's best to get your Christmas tree
out of the house before Valentine's
Day. Now is the time to do something
useful with it; turn it into a bird feeder.

It will provide some bird cover in
your back yard, and if you attach suet,
molded seeds or the hanging bird-food
"bells" you can find at most stores,
you'll help the bird.

If you don't want to feed the birds,
cutting off the limbs
of the tree will pro-
vide you with good
mulch for perennial
flower beds, espe-
cially fall-planted
mums.

If you were given
a living Christmas
tree, be sure to get
it in the ground by
early January and keep it well-watered.
Its roots won't have a chance to grow
in this weather and it could dry out and
die very quickly. Don't keep it in the
house for more than 10 days.

If possible, and this certainly depends
on the weather, keep watering your
evergreen plants, especially newly
planted ones. If the ground is frozen,
watch for the first available time to
water.

This is the time to decide if you want
to keep your Christmas plants or discard them. The Christmas pepper and
Jerusalem cherry will not flower again
and should be tossed out. But your
poinsettia, holiday cactus and cyclamen
should bloom until February or even
longer.

Give the poinsettia a sunny, cool location and water when the soil is dry.
About mid-March prune the stems from
3 to 6 inches to remove the colored
bracts, and fertilize the plant. Move it
outdoors in warm weather, and late
next September begin to alternate sun
and total darkness to induce blooming
again. You'll read more about that in
later chapters.

With cactus — and
this works for the
Thanksgiving cactus
as well as the
Christmas cactus —
give the plant a
sunny, cool home
indoors, water two to
four days AFTER the
soil is dry and fertil-
ize each month until
May.

Place it outdoors in June, water and
fertilize until August. About Sept. 1 cut
the watering in half, but try to leave the
cactus outdoors until about Oct 15. It
needs the cool nights to trigger the
flowering, but keep it protected from
frost. After Oct. 15, give it a sunny location indoors and enjoy the flowers.

You should be making periodic trips
around the yard checking young trees
for rodent damage on the lower trunks.

It's still not too late to protect them with hardware cloth or protective collars. There's nothing worse than to walk around the yard on the first nice day of spring and notice that the rodents have eaten the bark off your baby trees.

Although it's a little cold now to do much pruning of your trees and shrubs, it's never too soon to consider the proper tools you'll need and to make plans for doing the job properly.

For openers, you've got to have the right tools. You'll need hand pruners for the smaller branches, hand loppers for branches in the 1- to 2-inch range and a pruning saw for branches more than 2 inches. If you have a formal hedge, you'll need hedge trimmers. If you're handy enough, a chain saw is great for the bigger limbs or wind-damaged trees, but they are very dangerous. In the hands of an amateur, it's like using an ax to cut off a hangnail.

ALWAYS buy good tools. The cheaper ones may seem like a bargain, but you'll end up paying the price in dead or damaged shrubbery, all of it butchered with cheap or poorly sharpened tools. Plus, good tools last twice as long.

As will be repeated several times in this book, timing is very important when it comes to pruning. In general, you prune spring-flowering shrubs right after they bloom. The shrubs that bloom in the summer should be pruned in late winter or early spring. Prune very little in late summer; you could be encouraging new spurts of growth that will not "harden off" properly by fall.

When pruning an overgrown shrub, remember two things: Always maintain its natural shape, and -- unless it's become very leggy and badly in need of total renovation -- prune in moderation. Take two or three years to get it back in top shape. Always begin by pruning away the dead limbs, or those that "compete" with others.

When pruning shrubs, always cut back to within 1/4 inch of a bud, and angle the cut a little bit so the rain water will run off. Because a new branch always grows in the direction the bud points, always prune to an outward facing bud.

MIDDLE

If you're hungering for fresh blooms, early flowering trees and shrubs such as forsythia, crab apple, flowering quince, flowering dogwood and honeysuckle can be forced to bloom indoors by cutting off the branches and placing them indoors in warm water.

Since the seed catalogs come earlier every year, you should have a stack as high as the Christmas bills by now. We talk a lot about planning, but it's so vital to a well-landscaped lawn and healthy garden.

Think about what went wrong last year, what went right, and what you'd like to add or change. Draw detailed maps. Shut your eyes and see the even flow of colors, the subtle mix of evergreens and azaleas, the dogwood and the flowering pear. Then plan accordingly. Dreaming, at least, is free.

Check those stored canna, gladiolus,

dahlia and other tender bulbs you dug up last fall for signs of rot or excess moisture. Throw out the sick ones.

Try to increase the humidity around your houseplants, if not with watering pans then with a humidifier. A humidifier would be worth the investment if you plan to have healthy plants for a long time. It would keep you from drying up, too.

If you potted spring-flowering bulbs last October or November, you can bring a few out of cold storage now to begin the process of having them flower indoors. Place them in a cool, sunny area and add a little water.

LATE

This is the time of year when salt damage begins to show up on your plants as work crews salt the roads to make the drive home easier. The evidence is on the evergreen trees and bushes that show severe burn on one side, while the other side is deep forest green because the roots haven't been damaged.

Other indicators include stunting, dieback of the tips, leaf burn and leaf drop.

Some plants are more susceptible than others; cedars and white pines, for example, are more apt to be affected than Scotch and Austrian pines.

Among deciduous trees, oaks and sugar maples are more apt to be damaged, but the damage can't be seen until late in the spring when they leaf out.

Once the salt is in the trees, there isn't much you can do except try to keep the trees well-watered to leach out the salt. Be sure to fertilize them this spring.

Now is a good time to repot your root-bound asparagus fern, or the other ferns that seem to have stopped growing or are so thirsty they suck up every drop of water you give them in a few hours. You can grow the new divisions through the rest of the winter and surprise friends with a nice gift.

A pot-bound fern will have roots climbing all over the inside of the pot in a white mass. To help it, cut the rootball into halves, or even quarters, from top to bottom. Make clean cuts with a sharp knife to avoid too much root damage. Each slice should include a proportionate amount of foliage.

Gently untangle the matted roots so they will spread out in the new container. Place a few inches of sterile, well-drained potting soil in the new container and spread the root system over it. Fill in the rest, watering as you go to suck the soil down around the roots.

Remember those garden resolutions you made at the start of last season? Have you kept them? Have you taken your lawn mower or tiller to the shop for a tuneup? Don't forget to take extra blades for sharpening as well. A tuneup now will avoid weeks of waiting when it matters.

Are you saving your old motor oil to dump into a bucket of sand to clean your tools? And this year, buy a putty knife and keep it where you store the mower. Use it to clean the underside after every use. Disconnect the spark plug first.

FRED'S TIPS

Keep the leaves of your houseplants away from windows. One brush against frozen glass can injure, or even kill, your plants.

Here are some nifty tips I found in National Gardening magazine that will give you something to do this month, as well as help get rid of those ubiquitous plastic milk jugs. Save them and:

• Cut strips from the flat center portion to be used as plant labels.

Winter

• Cut off the bottom third of the jug for saucers or seed-starter trays.

• Cut off just the bottom surface to create a mini-greenhouse to protect new transplants in the garden.

• Remove the cap and cut off the bottom. Bury this "funnel" upside down next to a squash or pumpkin hill for fast, deep watering. Just fill the funnel and let the water trickle out.

You can also save those plastic, pint-sized berry baskets to protect newly sprouted seedlings in the spring, or use them to support melons and squash as they mature. It will keep them off the ground and away from bacteria.

You can also make your own seed tapes — those long strips of tape with seeds already attached at proper intervals—to kill sometime on a January day. It's the perfect thing to do with a child whom you're trying to interest in gardening.

All you need is seeds, flour and water, single-ply toilet paper and toothpicks. Make a flour and water paste thick enough to stick to a toothpick.

Roll out the paper. Spread seeds out on another piece of paper, dip the toothpick into the paste and then touch a seed. It will stick to the toothpick. Now place the seed on the toilet paper. Repeat this procedure, leaving the distance recommended on the seed package between the seeds. Let it dry, mark and store. When planted underground this spring, the paper and paste will disintegrate.

Try using sand, cat litter, ashes or even fertilizer as a de-icing agent on your sidewalk. Just don't overdo it; even they can cause damage. Too much fertilizer can be as unhealthy as too little.

If you don't have a "cold frame" to help you get the garden started early, give some thought to building one. It need not be elaborate; a square of treated lumber covered with plastic or an old storm window will do. But it can get your season started weeks earlier. You can also buy automatic openers for the cold frame lids that will prevent your plants from being fried on a sudden warm, sunny day. Check the catalogs and nurseries. If an opener saves one crop, it's almost paid for itself.

Here's another tip to occupy a winter weekend; try planting a terrarium— or "plants in a bottle." A terrarium can be fun, and because the plants provide their own environment, a terrarium is easy to care for— provided you get started correctly.

There are whole books on the subject, and you should buy one. Be sure to look around for exotic bottles, including the big ones once used for water supplies in company offices. Check the flea markets and antique stores.

I receive phone calls from newer gardeners periodically wanting me to clarify the meaning of "hybrid" in the seed catalogs.

Hybrid in a seed catalog means the first generation seed from a cross produced by combining two parent plants. It's done through controlled pollination to produce a new variety that is uniform and stable in the first generation.

These are called FI hybrids and must be created anew each year from crosses between breeding-stock parents. If you allow hybrid plants to go to seed and then plant that seed, you will not get many plants like the immediate parents. You get throwbacks to previous generations, which can be quite complex.

Therefore, every summer I get calls from gardeners wanting me to identify some strange-looking squash plant. I can't, because they planted seeds from hybrids grown the previous year. The offspring could look like anybody in the family.

Snow serves as an insulator and protects many plants from cold temperatures and drying winds. If it hangs on limbs, it must be removed very carefully — if at all — or you may break the limbs. Snow around the base of a bush, however, is a great help. Leave ice on tree limbs alone. It must melt naturally, or you'll damage the limbs.

I like to buy most of my seeds from local gardening centers, often after checking their colors and characteristics in the brightly colored catalogs we receive from seed companies.

If you do buy via the U.S. Mail, here are a few tips:

• Buy from a reputable firm.

• Don't be misled by fantastic claims; if it sounds too good to be true, it is. And fast-growing plants are often the weakest; a tree that goes up quickly often falls apart quickly. Read the descriptions carefully.

• Temperatures in our area sometimes fall to well below zero, so be sure to order plants hardy to this area.

• Keep a copy of your order. Pay by check or credit card. Keep track of the guarantee policy and use it.

You'll get more birds if you place your feeder near trees, shrubs or other natural cover. To that point, many people, myself included, have often said that if you begin feeding the birds, you shouldn't stop or they may starve.

But I received a letter from Dr. John S. Castrale with the Indiana Department of Natural Resources, who said there is no basis for believing that.

"Wintering birds are very opportunistic," he wrote, "and are attracted to feeders because food is available. If your feeder runs out of food, birds will look elsewhere. . ."

Castrale added that many people are afraid to begin feeding the birds because they think that if they stop or leave on vacation, the birds will die, which is not true.

What's important, he said, is to feed the birds during harsh weather, especially after a deep snow, and to buy quality seeds like those available from the local Audubon Society. Millet of various kinds, he said, should be the most important ingredient in commercially grown seeds.

FRED'S SUPER TIP

There's no part of gardening that requires more plain ol' trial and error than raising houseplants. The novice often runs into a bewildering array of warnings about too much light, not enough light, too much water, not enough water, too much fertilizer, etc.

Houseplants do take care, especially to keep them healthy indoors in the winter. But they're well worth the trouble. Here is a general outline of what to do.

Buy a good, general information book on raising houseplants, especially one that gives the light, temperature and water requirements of each plant. Whatever it costs, it will save you a lot of money.

All plants need light, and that can be easily supplied with artificial lights if the sun can't reach around the corner by the stairs. Be sure the light is no less than six to eight inches away and have

it on at least 16 hours a day. Just plain old cool-white fluorescent lights will work, and they're much cheaper than fancy plant lights.

Indoor houseplants can be invaded by pests almost overnight. A good magnifying glass will help you locate insects like scale, and there are insecticides you can use safely indoors in the winter. Read the labels carefully.

You must keep your plants clean, and that can be hard in the winter when the house is closed up. Take a damp cloth and wipe them off, give them a shower or even wash them with a safe soap and water; rinse well.

Because winter days are shorter and the light weaker, many plants like to rest from October through May. Let them do it. Feeding them fertilizer in the winter will only make them grow spindly.

This, of course, refers only to foliage houseplants. Those that bloom, like African violets, need to be fed regularly. Pay attention to the top soil. If it's too compact, take a fork and stir carefully and not too deeply. If it's crusty and white on top, you're getting too much mineral salt because the pot isn't draining properly. Check the drainage and rinse water through the plant. If the roots push out the bottom or are matted against the side of the pot, it probably needs repotting.

You never water houseplants on a regular basis, like once a week or once a month. There are too many variables: room temperature, the plant, the type of pot, etc.

Just feel the soil. When it feels dry to the touch, soak the plant until the excess water drains away. Never let the plant sit in water. That causes root rot. When the plant dries, water it again.

Houseplants like temperatures about 70 degrees in the day and 55 to 60 at night. Don't we all. Keep the plant away from drafts and heat radiators. At the Wiche house we like to use rubber trays filled with pebbles, which we water regularly to add humidity.

Keep in mind that all plants shed leaves occasionally, especially when they are moved. Some plants — like the popular weeping fig — hate to be moved; find a spot with good light and leave it there.

February

✏️ February Checklist

LAWN TIPS

☐ Last chance to get the lawn mower in good shape.
☐ Don't forget the soil test.
☐ Check the lawn for diseases.
☐ If you didn't fertilize in the fall, try a light application of high-nitrogen fertilizer now.

EARLY

☐ Order seeds, shrubs and trees from catalogs.
☐ Throw the groundhog a party to keep him above ground.
☐ Let sun melt ice on landscape plants.
☐ Try growing some plants in low-light areas.

MIDDLE

☐ Preserve the fresh-cut flowers you received for Valentine's Day.
☐ Fertilize fruit trees.
☐ Take soil sample for testing.
☐ Start broccoli, cabbage and cauliflower indoors.

LATE

☐ Begin dormant-spray program on trees, shrubs and roses.
☐ Check stored winter bulbs for rot. Begin fertilizing some houseplants.
☐ Apply pre-emergent crab-grass killer.
☐ Fertilize woody plants and bushes before new growth begins.
☐ Remove old asparagus and rhubarb tops and side-dress plants with ammonium nitrate.
☐ Clean out dead raspberry bushes.
☐ Begin pruning fruit trees.
☐ Fertilize spring bulbs as soon as they emerge from the soil.
☐ Check houseplants for spider mites.
☐ Sneak peas into the ground.
☐ Prune deciduous landscape plants.
☐ Prune grapes.

SUPER TIP

☐ Picking the perfect time to plant.

February may really be the cruelest month, that terrible 28- or 29-day interval between the time when it's way too cold to think about gardening and the time when you can begin "mudding in" peas or starting some spinach under clear plastic.

February comes from the Latin word *februare*, which means to purify. February was once the last month of the year, and those wild and crazy Romans used to purify themselves during February to get ready for the festivals in the coming year. February was made the second month in the calendar in 46 B.C. by Julius Caesar, who could do that kind of stuff.

The average high temperature in February is 45 degrees, and the average low is 26.8 degrees. The average precipitation in Kentuckiana in February is 3.23 inches, which includes melted snowfall. Ten inches of snow equals one inch of rain.

The warmest February day in Kentuckiana occurred on Feb. 10, 1932, when the temperature hit 78 degrees. The coldest was minus 19 on Feb. 2, 1951. The coldest temperature ever in Indiana was 35 below zero in Greensburg on Feb. 7, 1951.

The most Louisville-area precipitation was the 9.84 inches that fell in 1884; the least was .40 inches in 1947. Normal snowfall for the month is 4.7 inches.

There are 10 hours and 18 minutes of sunlight on Feb. 1, which increases to 11 hours and 20 minutes by the end of the month. The soil temperature in the area—taken at four inches below sod cover—ranges from 35 to 43 degrees.

Abraham Lincoln, Charles Lindberg and Ronald Reagan were born in February.

LAWN TIPS

This month — while you're still in your spring planning mode — we're going to talk about the types of grass that will work best for your lawn, including the endless quest for the perfect "shade grass." We'll also tell you what you can be doing in February to get your lawn ready for summer.

Please remember that February is not the best month to be planting grass; the job is best and most successfully done in August and September when there is less weed competition. The second best time is March.

Sowing grass seed on top of snow is an old wives tale that doesn't really work. We have fast melts here which carry the seed with them to drainage ditches or curb gutters. Also, seed won't germinate anyway until soils warm in April. By that time the seed will probably be lost to winds, rain, birds or trampled to death by the paper boy.

But often the new lawn must be planted in the spring. If you must sow seed now, please take a look ahead at the month of August for our complete, user-friendly, grass-planting instructions.

Meanwhile, just consider these AMAZING GRASS STATISTICS:

In a healthy, thick lawn there are about six to eight turfgrass plants per square inch, about 850 plants in a square foot and about 8 million plants in an average lawn of 10,000 square feet, or 35 million plants per acre.

You don't have to count them; please take our word for it.

A single plant can have 387 miles of roots, many of them, microscopic. So beneath this average, 10,000-square-foot lawn could lurk almost 3 billion miles of roots — the very reason why deep and thorough watering is so important.

Grassologists have also determined — somebody had to do it — that thick turfgrass will reduce the soil temperature 20 to 40 degrees in the summer. They've also learned that your average suburban lawn produces enough oxygen to meet the needs of a family of four, that each lawn traps hundreds of pounds of air pollutants, and that 90 percent of grass — by weight — is in its roots, making it a wonderful way to prevent erosion.

All grasses grow from seed. Most spread underground from "rhizomes," which are creeping stems that run horizontally under the surface of the soil. An exception is bluegrass, which grows by "stolons," above-ground runners that push up new grass shoots.

The most important part of the plant is the "crown," that bulging area right at the surface that is killed when you mow too close. That's a practice most delicately known as "scalping," and it makes the grass very vulnerable to disease or drought. That's why you should never mow more than one-third of your grass at once — and the top one-third at that.

The type of grass we use on our lawns depends primarily on climate, although shaded or very wet or dry areas can also be factors. Most people in the Kentuckiana area live in what's called the "transitional area" — it's often too hot in the summer for Kentucky bluegrass and too cold in the winter for such warm-season grasses as Bermuda grass and St. Augustine grass.

What kind of grass is best for your lawn? That depends on how much attention you want to give it. Kentucky is the bluegrass state, but a bluegrass lawn is like a rose garden; it's a very high-maintenance proposition that will surely feel the stress of summer heat. Bluegrass is not very good for high-traffic areas and is not well-adapted to medium or heavy shade.

The best overall answer for most home owners in Kentuckiana is the newer varieties of tall fescues now available, especially for people with soils that range from heavy clay to sand, or people who are trying to deal with light shade. Check with your nurseryman for the best varieties.

If you have a large, high-traffic area and do not care how course your lawn looks, the perennial favorite is Kentucky 31 fescue, a rough-looking grass that is tougher than green asphalt. All tall fescues are "loners" and should not be blended with other grasses.

Zoysia is a much talked-about grass because it is excellent for hot, dry summers and can take heavy wear. But keep three things in mind when deciding to sow it:

The grass will turn a straw color when dormant from October through mid-May; it doesn't like shade; it is very invasive. It will creep into your flower beds, or worse, your neighbor's yard. Once there, the only way to kill it is with a total-kill herbicide such as Roundup. And when planted by "plugs," it may take 10 years to get a zoysia lawn fully established.

But it is almost bulletproof when it gets established.

There are some other "speciality" grasses to consider, such as "fine fescues," which are tolerant of dry, poor, high-acid soils. They have finer leaves than the tall fescues but don't tolerate heavy traffic. "Perennial ryegrass" is very tolerant of traffic and can take compacted soil, but it has little heat tolerance and will often go dormant. It also tends to grow in "clumps" and should never be blended with tall or fine fescues.

What's the best thing to plant in medium to heavy shade?

My best answer is a picnic table. None of the grasses will work in dense shade — especially under maple trees with their invasive roots. If you plant early enough in the spring, you may think it's going to grow, but once the maple leaves pop out, the new grass inevitably suffers.

Tall fescues are somewhat shade-tolerant, and perhaps creeping red fescue might be some help, but I've never had any real luck with it. You might try pruning low branches to allow in some light, but maple-tree roots will suck up most of the water.

So consider a ground cover in heavier shade, plants such as ivy or vinca minor.

When buying your seed, be sure it says "certified" on the label and look for specific variety names such as Rebel or Falcon. Read the seed analysis tag before purchase and select only seed that has a very low percentage of weeds in it. Also, the higher the germination percentage, the better the seed.

If you are purchasing sod — which, if you can afford it, can make starting a new lawn so much easier — your best bet is "nursery-grown sod" that was grown specifically for transplanting. Pasture sod is exactly what the name implies — sod grown in some farm field. You'll get all the weeds and problems that come with it.

LAWN THINGS TO DO IN FEBRUARY:

Last chance to get the lawn mower in good shape before mowing begins.

Don't forget the soil test.

Check the lawn for diseases. It's too soon to use pre-emergent herbicides for crab grass and other weeds, but start looking for spring sales.

Late fall and early winter are the best times to apply fertilizer, but if you didn't get the job done last fall, one light application of high-nitrogen fertilizer will help.

Heavy fertilizing in the spring will promote a sudden flush of growth that will require more cutting. And it actually prevents your grass from establishing a better root system, which makes it less heat-tolerant come summer and more vulnerable to diseases.

GARDEN TIPS
EARLY

If you didn't order your seeds, shrubs or trees from the mail-order catalog —

and don't worry, they won't be shipped until you can plant them—you better finish the job. It's getting close to planting time.

Oh yeah; don't forget to include the shipping charges in your check; millions of us forget that every year. And don't order anything that can't survive in hardiness zone 5. Most of this area is actually in zone 6 — an area south of zone 5 —but it pays to be safe.

If this is the year you're going to order strawberries — after all those years of driving to someone else's patch to pick them — you better get to it. Spring is the best season to plant them.

Do everything you can to be sure the groundhog doesn't pop back underground for another six weeks of winter. Bake him a cake, throw a party or promise him a heated dog house. Let's keep that rascal above ground after Feb. 2.

Don't try to remove ice from landscape plants. Maybe you can slip some support beneath them, but let the sun melt the ice. That will prevent broken limbs.

I'm often asked this time of year about plants that will grow in low-light areas. There are plants that do especially well in homes with north-facing windows or with big shade trees out front.

The highest on my list is the Chinese evergreen. We have two varieties, and I think it's a very attractive plant that is badly underrated. You can also try the cast-iron plant, the vining pothos, the philodendron, the snake plant and last, but never least, the mother-in-law's tongue.

If you can't grow that, stick to plastic.

We've already talked a little bit about forcing some shrubs indoors to get some spring color early, but you might even go a step further and try forcing some more exotic plants like birch, oak or red maple limbs whose buds will be an indoor delight.

According to Southern Living magazine, you want to cut limbs that have plenty of buds and place them in a container of warm water. Store them where temperatures are between 60 and 65 degrees. Change the water every three or four days and cut an inch from the base of each stem every week until the flowers or foliage unfurl. It would make a nice show to go with forsythia or quince you've already forced indoors.

MIDDLE

Let's hope you received a bouquet of flowers for Valentine's Day. Let's hope they last at least as long as the thought behind them. Here's the way to make them last:

Flower stems that are not already in the water should be recut with a sharp knife as soon as they arrive. Remove at least a half-inch of stem so the flowers can better absorb water.

Remove any excess foliage that will be underwater. Use warm water; it will move more quickly into the flower. But let the flowers sit in tepid water for 20 minutes prior to arranging them. Roses are an exception; they prefer waiting in cold water before going in the warmer vase.

Use a commercial flower food or

preservative in the water. It contains sugar, acidifiers and a mild fungicide.

Avoid placing the flowers in excessive heat, such as in sunlight or on the television set. Place most flowers in a cool area — even the refrigerator — at night. Gladioluses and orchids should not be exposed to temperatures below 50 degrees. Happy Valentine's Day.

February is the month you want to fertilize fruit trees. Fruit trees should not be fertilized in late spring or early summer because that will prompt new growth that won't mature before frost.

For apple trees, apply 1/4 pound of ammonium nitrate for each year of the tree's age; for example, use one pound around a 4-year-old tree.

For peaches, plums and cherries, use 1/6 pound of ammonium nitrate per year, and for pears use 1/8 pound. Apply the fertilizer at the drip line of the tree (the outer reach of the lower branches), because roots will grow that far away from the trunk. Throwing fertilizer against the tree trunk is mostly a waste. Water the fertilizer in if nature doesn't quickly oblige.

You can also fertilize your other trees, using a high nitrogen mix like 27-3-3. But this is not mandatory. If you fertilized your lawn twice in the fall with a high-nitrogen fertilizer, your trees may not need much more. Check their health and see.

What's this? You still haven't taken a soil sample after years of being preached to about it? Get started now. Go to your local agriculture extension office and pick up your soil bags and instructions.

Remember: You may need to take several samples. If you want to plant rhododendrons or azaleas, they'll need an acid soil that won't do in the garden. Decide what plants you want where and learn their characteristics, then work on the soil samples. Spring is the best time to plant azaleas and rhododendron, as well as evergreens, because they lose so much water through their leaves during the winter.

It's time, believe it or not, to prepare for planting cool-weather seedlings such as broccoli, cabbage and cauliflower indoors. They can be started any time from mid-February to early March.

But hold off on starting warm weather plants such as tomatoes and green peppers. They don't go outdoors until early May, and if you begin them now, they'll get too big and leggy on you before you can get them outside — unless you have a well-equipped greenhouse.

Starting seedlings indoors can be very satisfying, but it takes a little work. To begin, find containers that will hold soil but drain easily. A milk container will do, or you can buy regular potting flats at the nursery.

Potting soil will work, but I prefer to use man-made soils like Jiffy-Mix or Ready-Earth. Fill the container with the planting medium, soak thoroughly and let it drain overnight.

Wet it again the next day, let it drain, sow your seeds ON TOP of the soil, then cover them with 1/16 inch of milled sphagnum moss.

Use a mister to soak the moss, let it drain again, then put the container in a clear plastic bag. Tie the end and put the container in a warm place, but not in direct sun.

It will take 24 for 36 hours for cole crops to sprout and five to 10 days for tomatoes or peppers. As soon as they do, remove the plastic bag and give them light and steady warmth. A window rarely works because the light is insufficient, and you will get thin, leggy plants.

The best light would be a bank of cool-white fluorescent tubes placed four to six inches above the seedlings. Move them up as the plants grow.

Keep the soil moist. In about 10 days, when the true leaves develop, feed them some fish emulsion fertilizer. As they get bigger, transfer them into individual Styrofoam cups. In about six weeks, move the plants outdoors gradually to harden them off. Plant them neck deep in the garden when they do get outside for good.

LATE

Contrary to what you might think, it's not too early to begin your dormant-spray program on outdoor trees, shrubs and roses. It's one of the most important things you can do for them all year.

Dormant oils coat the branches and trunks with a film that suffocates the aphids, mites and scale that spent the winter clinging to fruit and ornamental plants.

BE SURE to read the label carefully and apply only as directed. Also, be sure the temperature will be above freezing for at least 24 hours after the spray is applied, or it will not work.

Dormant oil shouldn't be used on everything, which is why you must read the label. For instance, it shouldn't be used on maples and could fade the blue color of your spruce.

Former University of Kentucky entomologist Dr. Rudy Scheibner reminds us that dormant oil is one of the safest sprays we use and can be used any time before new growth appears.

A dormant spray of lime sulphur diluted with water is also the best way to head off black spot disease on your roses. It's available at any gardening center.

Keep checking those stored winter bulbs for rot.

If your houseplants show signs of coming out of their winter doldrums, you might want to begin adding a little fertilizer to their water. In general, though, don't fertilize foliage houseplants until April. Also, keep picking off dead-looking leaves to encourage new growth.

Keep an eye on your forsythia bush, or maybe your neighbor's forsythia bush. It blooms just about the time you want to apply pre-emergent crab-grass killer to your lawn — sometime in late February to early March. Apply it a second time in May. You'll be so glad you

PRUNING FRUIT TREES

APPLE
(Central Leader Training)

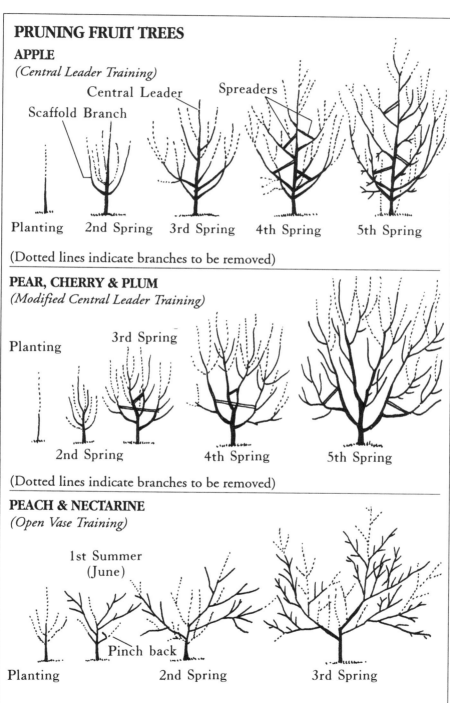

Central Leader Spreaders

Scaffold Branch

Planting   2nd Spring   3rd Spring   4th Spring   5th Spring

(Dotted lines indicate branches to be removed)

PEAR, CHERRY & PLUM
(Modified Central Leader Training)

Planting   3rd Spring

2nd Spring   4th Spring   5th Spring

(Dotted lines indicate branches to be removed)

PEACH & NECTARINE
(Open Vase Training)

1st Summer
(June)

Pinch back

Planting   2nd Spring   3rd Spring

(Dotted lines indicate branches to be removed)

applied it by July and August, when the crab grass normally attacks. But the pre-emergent needs rainfall or a good watering to get it into the soil. On many dry years it just sits there, and the crab grass grows anyway, thumbing its nose on the way past.

You can fertilize your woody plants and bushes with a high nitrogen fertilizer before new growth begins but after soil temperatures hit 40 degrees. You can check the temperatures with a soil thermometer or listen to agriculture reports.

If you haven't already done it, be sure to remove old asparagus and rhubarb tops and side-dress the plants with ammonium nitrate. Be sure to clean out the dead raspberry bushes if you didn't get to them last fall.

You can begin pruning fruit trees late in February. Start with the apples and leave the others until next month. When pruning apple trees, leave one strong leader or stem. Prune off competing upright limbs at the top of the tree. Then select three or four strong horizontal branches to save. Be sure they are evenly spaced around the trunk but not originating at the same level.

Fertilize spring bulbs as soon as they begin to emerge from the soil. Use a bulb-booster fertilizer or a 10-10-10 if you want to keep it simple. Don't worry about frost harming the bulbs. They are plenty hardy.

Double-check your houseplants for spider mites. Look for pale leaves and a very fine webbing encasing them. Wash

PRUNING GRAPEVINES

After 1st Growing Season

Before Pruning
After 2nd Growing Season

After Pruning

After 3rd Growing Season

After Pruning

the plants in lukewarm water or with insecticidal soap if it's a problem.

You can sneak your early peas into the ground in very late February. If you get a late start, however, you can jump-start the process by putting them in a plastic bag filled with wet sphagnum moss. Place it out of the sun but in a warm place, and in 24 hours they'll germinate, giving you a chance to catch up on a late planting.

You can also place some spinach seeds directly outdoors under a sheet of clear plastic to start them.

You can also prune your deciduous landscape plants now, but be sure you don't prune those that bloom in the spring such as forsythia, spirea and crab apple. Prune those right after the flowers fade.

Mid to late spring is the time to prune your grapes. It's not a terribly difficult task, but it must be done right if you want a decent grape crop every year. You'll be pruning off about 90 percent of last year's vines to get ready for this year.

FRED'S TIPS

If you're going to plant strawberries this year, consider using a pre-emergent weedkiller like Dacthal, which will help control weeds. It can be applied immediately after planting or any time during the first season if you're not going to eat the berries. Dacthal works well on many fruits and flowers, including the iris, which always causes weeding problems. You can use Dacthal now, but please, please read the label; it might injure some other crops.

Bill Young, a friend of mine who has worked for years in the agriculture and horticulture chemical industry, put it best: "We don't put labels on boxes, bags and bottles of chemicals for decoration — they are there to protect your health, as well as the health of your plants."

When you order trees and shrubs by mail, you might be surprised to learn that many come bare-rooted — without a hint of dirt on the roots. That's fine, as long as the plants are dormant. If you can't plant them right away, dig a trench and cover the roots until you can.

Twenty-four hours before planting, soak the roots of bare-root trees or bushes and plant directly into the hole. Spread out the roots. Don't be afraid to prune off the broken or injured roots.

When planning your garden, you should rotate your five main crop groups from year to year to help disease control. The groups are the nightshade family, which includes potatoes, tomatoes, eggplant and peppers. The second group is vine crops, such as cucumbers and melons. The third is corn and green manure crops, such as rye and wheat. The fourth is crucifers, such as cabbage, broccoli and cauliflower. The fifth is legumes, such as peas, along with beets and carrots.

If you have a deciduous hedge, like a privet, that's gotten too tall and scraggly due to improper pruning, it should be cut down to about six inches so it can start over again. Once the hedge has been cut back, fertilize it with a 10-10-10 mix; two to four pounds per 100 square feet. Next time prune it right; be sure the top is narrower than the bottom so the sun can get to it.

Avoid blowing or shoveling snow onto your plants. Snow, especially heavy, wet spring snow, can smash them. If there's no where else for the snow to go, wrap the plants in burlap to help them stand up.

Here's the best way to tell if your plant is pot-bound. Place one hand over the top of the pot, fingers around the stem to hold the soil in place. Invert the plant and tap the pot against the edge of the table. If the soil ball that emerges shows a thickly matted mass of roots, it's time to repot. Make sure your new pot is an inch or two larger than the old. Gently pry the root mass apart before replanting, trimming away excess roots as you go.

Horse or cow manure can make a great compost, especially when mixed with straw or saw dust. But for best results let it sit under black plastic for a year to kill the weeds and to let the manure settle out. The ammonia in fresh manure can kill a plant.

Here are a dozen trees the University of Kentucky says should not be planted in the urban home landscape because they are either too weak, have invasive roots, produce messy fruit or have too many suckers: catalpa, silver maple, mulberry, Lombardy poplar, tree of heaven, osage orange, box elder, European white birch, cottonwood, black locust, Siberian elm and willows.

FRED'S SUPER TIP

You will notice that the information at the beginning of each chapter includes average soil temperatures for the month around Kentuckiana. Those figures will fluctuate every year and are only intended as general indicators.

Ground temperatures, like air temperatures, can fluctuate as much as 20 to 30 degrees a day near the surface. But as you go 20 inches underground, the temperature may fluctuate only one degree in a day.

In most years, the average soil temperature is the lowest in mid-January and early February; often in the mid 30s. It's warmest in late July and early August, often in the low 80s.

Official Kentucky ground temperatures are taken four inches below sod, which provides a constant all tracking stations use. The bare soil in your garden, of course, will be several degrees warmer than it is four inches below sod.

It's important to know this because many plants have minimum temperatures below which seeds will not germinate. In a particularly cold, wet spring, the seed could rot.

Although the time when the soil reaches a certain optimum temperature may vary from year to year, the annual cycle is usually consistent. Heavy rains and wet soil may delay the warming, but rarely by more than one or two weeks.

So it pays to keep track of soil temperatures, either with a thermometer or by monitoring farm reports. For instance, it's known that the minimum temperature for corn germination is about 50 degrees, but germination would be very slow at that temperature. The optimum is 60 degrees and above, but when the temperature hits 107 — not unusual in a bare field in midsummer — it's too hot for germination.

Tomato sets make their best growth when soil temperatures hit 85 degrees, an easy temperature to find during a summer day, although it may drop below that at night. Tomato growth is very slow at 55 to 60 degrees.

So here then is a brief list of the MINIMUM temperatures needed for the following vegetables to germinate: asparagus, 50 degrees; beets, 40 degrees; cabbage, 40 degrees; carrots, 40 degrees; cucumbers, 60 degrees; lettuce, 35 degrees; onions, 35 degrees; peas, 40 degrees; radishes, 40 degrees; squash, 60 degrees; melons, 60 degrees.

Knowing that should help with planting.

March

◉▷ March Checklist

LAWN TIPS

❑ Seed your lawn if you didn't do so in the fall.
❑ Start mowing now for a healthy, properly manicured lawn.
❑ If the forsythia are blooming, it's time to use a pre-emergent herbicide to control crab grass.
❑ If you wish to control broadleaf weeds chemically, begin using herbicides that contain 2,4-D and MCPP.
❑ This is the month to lime your soil.

EARLY

❑ Force forsythia and pussy willow to bloom indoors.
❑ Plan vegetable and flower gardens.
❑ Prepare soil near house for small salad garden.
❑ Sharpen shears and checks rakes and hoes.
❑ Plant rhubarb.

MIDDLE

❑ Plant cool-season crops such as cabbage, brussels sprouts, turnips, peas, carrots, lettuce, cauliflower, broccoli, kohlrabi and collards.
❑ Examine transplants for disease.
❑ Protect transplants from cutworms.
❑ Transplant cool-season flowers outdoors.
❑ Finish spraying fruit trees and berry plants with dormant oil.
❑ Examine leftover pesticides for signs of age or damage.
❑ Apply pre-emergent herbicides to flower beds and vegetable garden.
❑ Plant asparagus.

LATE

❑ Remove flower stalks from spring-flowering plants and fertilize beds.
❑ Cut back liriope before new growth begins.
❑ Divide perennials and plant new ones.
❑ Fertilize houseplants every other week.
❑ Start caladiums indoors.
❑ Spray pine trees suffering from scale.

SUPER TIP

❑ Think small when planting fruit trees.

March is the time when winter finally melts into the magic of springtime bulbs, high school basketball turns into March Madness, and the NCAA playoffs begin. What could be better than that?

March is named for Mars, the Roman god of war, who probably tore up a lot of gardens in his day.

The average high temperature is 54.9 degrees, and the average low is 35.2, with plenty of nasty freezes left, so don't get in too big a hurry to plant.

The average March precipitation is 4.73 inches, but sometimes that all comes at once. Some 14.97 inches of precipitation fell in March 1964, including a gully-washing 6.97 inches on March 9, producing what's lovingly known as the '64 Flood. The least precipitation ever in March was in 1930 when only .12 inches fell.

The highest temperature ever in March was 88 degrees, which occurred twice: March 22, 1907 and March 25, 1929. The coldest was a nose-tweeking 1 degree below zero on March 6, 1960, which must have surprised a lot of potatoes.

March, 1960 was a dandy. It produced 18 inches of snow in Bowling Green on March 9, the state record for one day. It dumped 46.5 inches of snow on Benham in Harlan County, a state record for one month. Poor Benham had 96.7 inches of snow that year. As comparison, the normal snow in Louisville for March is 3.9 inches.

There are 11 hours and 21 minutes of possible sunlight on March 1, but we rarely get that much. By March 31 the sun is up 12 hours and 35 minutes.

The average soil temperature — at a depth of four inches below sod — ranges from 45 to 52 degrees.

Knute Rockne, the famous Notre Dame football coach with the "golden thumb," was born March 4, 1888. Julius Caesar, the man who could move months, was assassinated March 15, 44 B.C.— so beware the Ides of March.

LAWN TIPS

Oh, boy. It's already March, the daffodils are sending up fountains of bright yellow flowers, the NCAA basketball season is winding down to a Final Precious Four, and your lawn is winding up for the long, hot summer.

Here's what you can be doing in March.

SEEDING YOUR LAWN — As we explained in February, spring is not the best time to seed, but it may be the best time you have. You'll find complete seeding instructions in the August section. Grass won't germinate unless the soil temperatures hit the low 60s, so if it's been a cold spring, you're wasting your time planting now.

FERTILIZE THE LAWN — Again, fall is the best time, but a light fertilizing of a care-starved lawn isn't all bad. Use a high-nitrogen fertilizer, but remember: Too much spring growth above ground means a weaker root system below ground and diseases down the road.

I've also never been a big fan of the

spring "weed and feed" concept. Many of the weeds you're trying to kill, like dandelions, haven't even emerged yet, so you can't kill them, and you already know too much spring fertilizer is a bad idea.

MOWING THE LAWN — It never seems quite fair that lawn mowing and NCAA basketball should coincide, but they often do. Your lawn's early growth is often raggedy — let's face it, it's often ugly — but it needs to be kept as even as possible. Your newly sharpened, well-tuned lawn mower should handle it with ease. Early in the season mow the grass to about 2 to 2 1/2 inches in height, and you should never let it get more than 4 inches tall, although that often seems unavoidable in the rainy season.

If it does get tall, don't take off all that extra growth at once. Raise the mower an inch above normal and mow, then lower it to the normal height in a few days and do it again. As a general rule of thumb, never cut off more than a third of your grass; anything beyond that can send it into "shock," allowing weeds and bugs to move in.

Later on in the year, as temperatures rise, you'll want to mow your grass to about 2 1/2 to 3 inches to help protect it from the heat.

For years many homeowners have been catching their clippings in a side basket and putting them in the garbage — along with leaves — to be taken to landfills, which are filling up.

Modern research has shown that grass clippings contain 75 to 85 percent water and easily decompose. If the lawn is cut a little more frequently — every five to seven days in the spring — and if the lawn mower is kept sharpened, the decaying grass clippings actually help the lawn by returning nitrogen and nutrients to the soil.

In fact, "mulching mowers," which distribute clippings evenly across your lawn, are now being promoted as a way to improve the lawn. The newer mulching or recycling lawn mowers cut and recut clippings, allowing them to decay more easily.

Contrary to popular opinion, the dreaded "thatch" buildups in bluegrass lawns are not caused by grass clippings but by over-fertilized, overwatered lawns that cause the old grass stems and roots to pile up at the soil surface. And remember this: Thatch is primarily a problem in bluegrass lawns; it's not a problem with tall fescues.

One last mowing point: Don't let your lawn go into winter more than 2 inches in length. As long as the grass grows, you have to mow it, but it's a lot healthier and happier going into the cold season with a short haircut.

PRE-EMERGENT HERBICIDES FOR CRAB GRASS — Although the dreaded crab-grass invasion will not occur until the hot, humid days of July, now is the time to control it. There are a half-dozen varieties of pre-emergent herbicides, granular chemicals that go on the lawn now and kill the crab-grass seed before it germinates. In most parts of Kentucky they must be applied before April 1, although they can be used in Northern Kentucky and Southern Indiana until April 15. The general rule of thumb I use is that when the forsythia are blooming, it's time for the crab-grass killer. It's available at any garden center. Be sure to follow the directions very carefully. If you are seeding a lawn, only certain pre-emergent crab-grass control can be used. Be sure to read the label thoroughly before you buy the product.

One warning, however: Pre-emergent herbicides have only a limited window of opportunity to work. Weather factors, such as a very rainy period, will increase the breakdown of the pre-emergent and allow increased crabgrass germination. Crab grass will be killed by the first heavy frost in the fall, so fertilize your "wanted" grass after that and try pre-emergent again the following spring.

WEED CONTROL OF OTHER BROADLEAF WEEDS — The dandelions, plantains, clover, chickweed and henbit that remain pests long after the crab grass has been sent packing can be controlled with broadleaf herbicides that contain 2, 4-D and MCPP. Again, use these very carefully and only when the air is still; they are also very deadly to some ornamentals. On a newly seeded lawn, mow twice before using a broadleaf herbicide.

If you have the dedication, many broadleaf weeds can be removed by hand with hoes, trowels or those long-handled dandelion removers.

SOIL SAMPLES — We've done a lot of preaching about taking soil samples from your lawn, and you know they are important, so you'll know exactly what type of fertilizer, or how much lime, to purchase.

But how is it done?

Here are the directions provided by the Jefferson County (Kentucky) extension office (in Indiana, check with your extension service):

Start in one corner of the lawn soil to be sampled. Take a small "plug" of dirt from that area to a depth of about 3 inches, being sure not to include grass or weeds. Take about 10 to 15 such samples from around your yard. If you do it carefully, replacing your divots as you go, your yard doesn't have to look like Limburger cheese. In fact, it shouldn't look damaged at all.

Spread the soil out on a piece of paper and let it dry for two days at room temperature, then mix the dry soil together thoroughly. Next take about a pint of the soil in a clean container to your extension office for testing. There will be a slight cost — often about $3 to $4 — and you'll get the results in a few weeks.

You can and should do the same things for your vegetable, flower and shrub gardens, but in those instances you want to take your samples from about 6 inches deep in the ground.

SELECTING A LAWN-CARE COMPANY — With so many men and women working these days, and the children off to their various summer camps and programs, more and more people are turning their lawns over to lawn-care companies.

To help families decide which services are best and how much lawn care is really needed, Dr. A. J. Powell Jr., a turf specialist at the University of Kentucky Extension, has written a checklist of things to consider.

Ironically enough, says Powell, very often "high-maintenance programs" — those that provide four or five fertilizer applications and three to four herbicide applications a year — will actually make lawns more susceptible to weather stress and pests.

That's because, Powell said, these overly cared-for lawns tend to develop thick layers of thatch; an organic layer of dead grass that will develop between the soil surface and the green vegetation, causing shallow root systems.

He also said the homeowner must keep his or her part of the bargain by mowing and watering the lawn on schedule, or the overfertilized lawn will go nuts, producing lush top growth at the expense of the roots.

He recommended a more moderate approach to the use of fertilizers in the spring, not only for environmental reasons but because grasses in our transitional growing area tend to become tougher when left a little more to their own devices.

In selecting a lawn-care company, Powell said to check out a company's reputation within the community, ask the salesman or applicator how much training he's had and be careful about being oversold; more is not necessarily better.

He also said it's best to have a company where consultation is only a phone call away and to observe — when possible — the company's employees at work to be sure they're doing a good job in all the applications.

Remember, Powell cautioned, that lawn-service companies vary in their competence, that their efforts are a "joint effort" with your efforts, and that if you don't intend to water or mow correctly between visits, you're better off without them.

LIMING THE SOIL — Most homeowners lime their soil about as often as they hit the Kentucky or Indiana lottery. Lime is important; it helps lower the acidity of the soil, and lower acid means the sweeter soil can better accept and use the nutrients in the fertilizer.

Again, your soil test will tell you how much lime your lawn needs, if any. Fall is the best time to lime, but spring is OK, especially for lawns that have been limed for many years. Lime is best spread evenly by a spreader, not tossed by hand about the lawn in great white clouds, which could make you more "sweet" than your soil.

GARDEN TIPS
EARLY

Although they'll be blooming outdoors any time, you can still "force" forsythia or pussy willow to bloom indoors. Go out to the bush, snip off a few extraneous limbs, then place the cuttings in warm water. In a few days you'll have a little touch of spring blossoming in your house.

If you haven't planned your vegetable or flower gardens, it's past time to get started. Draw up a rough plan of what you want, being sure to rotate crops to a different spot from where they were last year. Remember, smaller plants should be grown in front of the taller ones so they will have sufficient sunlight. For vegetables, that's at least six hours a day.

If you want a small area near the house in which to begin a salad garden, you can lay a sheet of clear plastic on the ground and hold it down with bricks. That will warm and dry the soil, giving you a head start.

But don't be overanxious to plant. Test the soil by squeezing it with one hand. If it crumbles and slips through your fingers, the soil is ready to work. If it wads up like a ball of putty, it's still too early to plant.

Pruning season means you must have sharp tools. A well-sharpened pair of shears should cut through a facial tissue or a single sheet of newspaper. If your shears aren't that sharp, find a good sharpening service and get them honed. You'll be glad you did, and so will your plants. Check the condition of your rakes, shovels and hoes while in the garage.

If you have your heart set on rhubarb-strawberry pie, early to mid-March is the best time to plant the rhubarb part of that delicious combination.

Rhubarb thrives in a sunny location in fertile, well-prepared soil. Work the soil as soon as you can. Incorporate peat moss, compost or well-rotted manure. Set the new plants (crown and bud side up) three to four inches deep and about three to four feet apart. Water deeply during dry spells and fertilize in midsummer and early each spring.

Do not harvest any rhubarb the year you plant it. Starting the second year, you can harvest for about six weeks in spring and early summer. Grab the large outer stalks near their base and twist them off. Do not pull more than two-thirds of the stalks off any plant. Throw away all leaves because the foliage is poisonous.

I recently noticed an article in the "Victory Garden Landscape Guide" that should be of interest to many gardeners. It was about the use of "native plants" in the home landscape.

The point of the article is that too often gardeners will fight to place an exotic ornamental shrub or tree on their lawn only to see it suffer — or even die — because it just doesn't belong there.

By using native plants, the ones native to your area, you're almost guaranteed to get trees and shrubs that work. That doesn't mean you'll not find interesting trees for your yard.

The sourwood tree, for example, will rival the dogwood for year-round beauty. The yellowwood tree, which has lovely hanging bunches of fragrant white flowers many years, is also native to this area but is rarely found in home landscapes.

Look around. Some nurseries even specialize in native plants and trees.

According to the "Victory Garden" book, some of the more interesting native trees in this area include the serviceberry, sassafras (Japanese beetles love them), American beech, black gum, scarlet oak, Carolina silverbell, fringe tree and shagbark hickory.

Some native shrubs include the red chokeberry, witch hazel, sumac and highbush cranberry. Evergreen trees and shrubs include American holly, red cedar, white pine and inkberry. For vines, try the trumpet vine, bittersweet or Virginia creeper.

MIDDLE

Mid-March is the time to plant cool-season crops such as cabbage, brussels sprouts, turnips, peas, carrots, lettuce, cauliflower, broccoli, kohlrabi and collards.

For best results, cabbage, brussels sprouts, cauliflower and broccoli should be grown from transplants The others can be grown from seeds.

Examine the transplants for disease before planting. Look for galls, ash-gray leaf spots and cankers. Discard any that look sickly. The best transplants are often the stocky ones with the thick stems.

Cabbage and other cole crops are susceptible to cutworms which are often found in gardens where there had been grass the year before. Cutworms literally cut the plants off at the ground line and don't even bother to holler "timmmberrrr."

Paper collars wrapped around the plants' stems will prevent cutworm damage, or you can buy cutworm bait at a seed store. Diazinon powder that you wet may be used on the soil prior to setting out transplants to protect them against cutworms and root maggots.

Although we don't often think of flowers in March, cool-season flowers such as snapdragons, pansies, ornamental cabbage, dwarf carnations, pinks, primrose and sweet williams should be transplanted outdoors during mid- to late March, with March 20 considered about the best time most years. These flowers will need at least five hours of sun a day and are tough enough to sustain a light frost.

You are running out of time to effectively spray fruit trees and raspberry plants with dormant oil to protect them against diseases like peach-leaf curl, plum pockets and anthracnose.

You'll find more complete in formation on spraying with dormant oil in the February chapter, but that's only the first job in what can be a season-long battle against bugs and diseases.

If you are serious about raising good fruits and berries, contact the nearest Kentucky Cooperative Extension Service office and ask for a copy of brochure ID 21, "Pest Control Program for Home-Grown Fruit in Kentucky." It does a much better job of explaining the complex spraying program than I can in a limited space. Persons living in other states should get a similiar brochure from their state agents.

Pesticides purchased last year, or pesticides that were stored in the garage over the winter, should be examined for signs of age or damage.

Sludge-like material at the bottom, cracks in the containers, bulges in the sides and strong odors are indicators the pesticides have been damaged. If all indications are bad, the pesticide should be thrown out. The Environmental Protection Agency says wrap them deep in newspapers and discard them in the garbage.

Perhaps one of the most important steps you can take in mid-March is to kill weed seeds as they germinate by working pre-emergent herbicides into the soil as you prepare the beds.

Both Treflan and Dacthal are suitable for use in flower beds and the vegetable garden. Be absolutely sure to use only as directed on the label. Also, remember that a pre-emergent cannot be used in all parts of a vegetable garden. Some crops, such as corn, can be damaged by pre-emergent herbicides, so you'll have to leave an untreated area for some vegetables.

Asparagus, like rhubarb, can be planted in mid-March. It grows best in full sun, maybe at the north or west side of your garden where it won't be disturbed or shaded by vegetables. Also, keep in mind that it will grow four to six feet high and would make a nice screen. It also grows well along a fence.

Asparagus must have well-drained

soil. Dig a trench 12 inches deep and 15 inches wide. Add generous amounts of compost, peat moss and well-rotted manure to a depth of about six inches. Then add about 1/4 cup of 5-20-20 fertilizer per plant.

Plant roots that are one year old, allowing a dozen for each member of your family. Set the roots at the bottom of the trench, which is now about six inches deep; the plants should be about 18 inches apart. Be sure the crowns are facing up. Cover the roots with three to four inches of soil but not all the way to ground level. Then fill in the trench gradually as the shoots grow, always leaving the tips exposed. Every fall, after the top growth is cut back, mulch over the top of the bed. This eventually produces a long ridge.

New research indicates that some light cutting can be made for about four weeks the spring after planting. In the second year, a normal eight-week cutting period can be started.

LATE

After the blossoms of spring-flowering bulbs have faded, cut off the spent flower stalks, then feed the plants with 1/2 cup of 5-10-10 fertilizer per 10 square feet of bed if you didn't do it earlier. The best time to feed the bulbs is when the foliage is breaking through the ground.

Do not remove the foliage after the flower fades; it's needed to replenish the underground bulb. Once the foliage begins to yellow naturally, it's fine to remove it.

You can rejuvenate your liriope (monkey grass) by using a lawn mower to cut back the old foliage to 3 or 4 inches. This should be done before new growth begins. If your plant has started new growth, be sure to cut above it.

If you didn't get to divide your perennials last fall, or you'd like to plant more, there's still time. Choices for sunny areas include day lilies, yarrow, Shasta daisies, perennial phlox and coneflowers. Shade-loving perennials include columbines, hostas and ferns.

As warmer weather approaches, it's time to think about feeding your houseplants every other week with a water-soluble fertilizer like 18-18-18 or 20-20-20. A lot depends on the weather, but late March to April is the time to wake up your houseplants and get them ready to be moved outside.

While you're waking things up, caladiums, which produce marvelously showy leaves all summer, are best started indoors to get their engines running. Start them in flats or pots that are at least 30 percent sphagnum moss or compost. Plant the tubers about an inch deep in bright, indirect light. Keep them moist. When the outdoor soil temperature is about 60 degrees, move them outdoors. To encourage fuller growth, remove the center tuber as it develops.

If your pine trees have taken on a different color, looking almost a ghostly white, it isn't paint; it's an insect called scale. Scale is especially bad on low-growing pines. It spends the winter under those white spots, then emerges in spring to suck vital juices from the needles. It can be controlled with a lime-sulphur dormant spray applied when temperatures are above freezing for 24 hours. Later in the summer an insecticide like Orthene or Isotox will control scale.

FRED'S TIPS

A few years ago I received a great tip from a Mount Washington, Ky., woman for protecting baby plants during cold weather. She said that as she sets out broccoli, cauliflower and brussels sprouts, she covers each plant with a paper cup with the bottom cut out. On extra-cold nights, she covers that cup with another cup with the bottom left in it. The first cup allows sun through the top. The second keeps out the cold.

March is a good time to bath houseplants in hot water to get them ready to go outdoors in the spring. Begin by filling a sink or tub with liquid or flake soap; don't use detergent because it is too strong. Put the pot in a plastic bag, drawing the top of the bag around the base of the plant so the dirt doesn't spill into the slnk.

Turn the container upside down and

swish the foliage around in the soapy water. If you think spider mites have attacked your plant, don't rinse the leaves; the soap provides some protection. If there are no insects, go ahead and rinse the plant. Most plants, with the exception of fuzzy-leafed varieties such as African violets, or ferns, cactus and succulents, like a bath three or four times a year.

If you have shady areas in your yard but still want some colorful understory trees in those areas, consider the dogwood, redbud and Canadian or Carolina hemlock. For shrubs, consider the glossy abelia, Oregon grape holly or witch hazel. All plants need some light to grow, but these will tolerate shade as long as it isn't as dark as the inside of a closet.

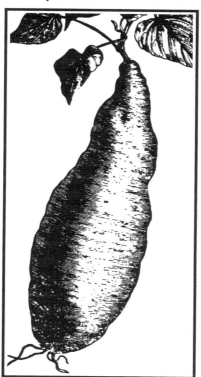

The roots of a walnut tree give off a toxic material that is injurious to many plants. Try a raised-bed garden in those areas, but only if you plant shallow-rooted plants such as lettuce and impatiens that also tolerate shade. Deep-rooted plants may come in contact with walnut roots. Also, remember that a raised bed that is too big might injure tree roots.

A sun box made of aluminum foil can brighten your prospects for growing straight and sturdy transplants indoors when the sun is scarce.

Set plants in a large cardboard box with the front cut out and the back lined with aluminum foil. When placed near windows, the foil lining reflects the light back onto the plants, and stems grow straight instead of leaning toward the sun.

The sun box is reusable year after year. Leftover aluminum strips can be placed at the base of squash plants where the reflected light will discourage bugs that like to lay eggs in the normally dark stem area. Aluminum foil placed around a garden has also been known to discourage night-prowling bunnies.

The carrot is another vegetable that will benefit from having seeds soaked in water for a few hours before planting. One year, on the advice of a friend, I poured the carrot seeds into a sprinkling can, then walked up and down a row sprinkling and sowing at the same time.

After several days, when nothing came up, I told my friend his idea didn't work. He told me to take the nozzle off my can.

I did. There were the seeds. If you try this, be sure the holes in the can are large enough to allow the seeds to pass through.

When cutting up seed potatoes before planting, it's best to let them heal for about 24 hours so the pieces can "scar" over. Be sure to get at least one eye in each piece or the potato will never see its way to the top.

Get them in as early as possible. You can bury them about six inches deep and a few feet apart, although some people have had great luck growing potatoes under nothing but a straw mulch. Even if you bury them, straw mulch is a good idea.

The insecticide Thiodan has been successful against the dreaded Colorado potato beetle in recent years, but the beetles are now showing signs of becoming immune to that. What's a gardener to do.

If you're just beginning to garden and are in need of some "sure-thing" annual flowers, the specialists at the University of Kentucky say begonias, periwinkles, ornamental peppers, impatiens and coleus do best in the Kentuckiana climate. All do well in the garden or in containers.

In the absence of a soil test, you can get by in your garden by applying 25 pounds of 5-10-10 or 6-12-12 fertilizer per 1 ,000 square feet of gardening area. That's about 2 1/2 pounds per 100 square feet. Add two tablespoons of 5-10-10 fertilizer or 6-12-12 per bushel of soil for container growing.

Early spring, after the serious frost has departed but before the temperatures rise into the 50s and 60s, is the best time to prune grapes. There are several ways of doing this depending on space and variety.

The best advice I can give is to find a publication showing how a properly pruned grape arbor should look. Your local extension service or garden-supply store should have it. This is very important because about 90 percent of a grape arbor is pruned each year, and you have to know which 90 percent.

FRED'S SUPER TIP

If you are thinking about adding fruit trees to your garden this year, let me give you one piece of advice: Think small.

There's room in almost every home garden for dwarf or semi-dwarf apple trees; be sure to buy at least two or they'll not pollinate. Not only do these trees require less space, but they can be pruned, thinned, sprayed and harvested from the ground or with the use of a small ladder. They may cost more initially, but they will save money in the long run.

When it comes to cherry trees, all we have in our garden is "Northstar Dwarf" and "Montmorence Dwarf." I would never have a standard cherry tree because the birds get most of the harvest. Our trees are only seven to eight feet tall, and when the cherries ripen we can cover them with fruit-tree netting

and get our full harvest. If you're thinking about cherry trees, buy only tart;
sweet cherries will rarely develop a
crop in this part of the country.

Fruit trees should be fertilized now,
not in late spring or summer. An apple
tree requires 1/4 pound of ammonium
nitrate for each year of the tree's age.
Peaches, plums and cherries use 1/6
pound for each year, and pears use 1/8
pound. Spread the fertilizer below the
drip line of the tree, not up against the
trunk.

One final thought on trees: Spend a
little money and buy the most disease-
resistant varieties available. You don't
want to spray them with fungicides all
summer. Among apple trees, the
disease-resistant would include Liberty,
Freedom, Prima, Priscilla, Jonafree and
Redfree.

April

✏️ April Checklist

LAWN TIPS

❑ A happy lawn is a well-mown lawn.
❑ Use pre-emergent crab-grass killers and chemical broadleaf weedkillers early this month if you have not already done so.
❑ Water your lawn deeply and on a regular basis.

EARLY

❑ Start warm-weather crops indoors.
❑ Fertilize, prune and spray rose bushes.
❑ Check tulip bed for tulip fire disease.
❑ Plant carrots and radishes.
❑ Check tubers and corms of gladioluses and cannas.
❑ Start tuberous begonias indoors.
❑ Apply weedkiller to wild garlic.
❑ Take wrapping off trees planted last fall.
❑ Plant new trees.

MIDDLE

❑ Plant snap and lima beans.
❑ Prune spring-flowering shrubs after blooms fade.
❑ Start transplants for muskmelon and watermelon.
❑ Check strawberry plants.
❑ Fertilize magnolias.
❑ Prune peach trees.
❑ Fertilize trees.

LATE

❑ Check vegetable garden for aphids.
❑ Protect vegetable garden from rabbits.
❑ Blanch cauliflower.
❑ Prune peony buds. Fertilize evergreens.
❑ Check trees for tent caterpillars.

SUPER TIP

❑ How to start seeds in a bag.

April is the month we've all been waiting for. The tulips are up and hoping to make it to Derby Week — and so are we. But caution is advised. Although the last average frost date in this area is in early April, that varies greatly from year to year, and it's still too early to plant the more sensitive plants.

April apparently takes its name from the Latin word *aperire*, which means "to open." There is another school of thought that says it was named for Aphrodite, the Greek goddess of love, and that makes sense too.

The average high temperature in April is 67.5 degrees; the average low is 45.6 degrees. The average precipitation is 4.11 inches, which means more rain normally falls in March, even if we think of April showers in song and story.

A record 11.10 inches of rain fell in Louisville in March 1970. (They started keeping records in the 1870s.) The least-ever April rain was .25 inches in 1896, a good spring for dry humor.

The warmest April day ever was April 23, 1925, and April 24, 1960, when the temperature hit 91 degrees. The coldest day was April 18, 1875, when it was 21 degrees, and that must have tested some peach crops.

The average snowfall in the Louisville area for April -- a statistic that rarely wears out the weatherman's pencil — is .2 inches.

There are 12 hours and 37 minutes of possible sunlight on April 1, and 13 hours and 45 minutes by April 30. The average soil temperature ranges between 52 and 59 degrees.

The Indian Pocahontas, who had something to do with home-grown Thanksgiving dishes, married John Rolfe on April 5, 1614, and the Pony Express began on April 3, 1860, probably to deliver seed catalogs.

LAWN TIPS

April is the wonderful month when the dogwoods bloom, the flowering crabs and redbuds fill the air with explosions of red and pink, and the green, green grass begins to take its mission in life seriously.

It's your mission to keep it in its place.

More than half of all grass mowing normally takes place in April and May. Usually we try to mow the grass at about 2 to 2 1/2 inches in height this time of year, but sometimes you might have to raise the blade to about 3 inches and come back in a few days, lower the blade and cut it back to the proper height.

That prevents so many clippings on the surface. These shorter clippings can better decay into the grass rather than having to be raked up and sent to the landfills — which are already filling up too fast. Clippings are actually very helpful to your lawn if your mower spreads them uniformly and not so thickly that they shade or smother the grass.

According to the University of Kentucky, grass clippings are not the culprits in thatch buildup we suspect.

Grass clippings contain 75 to 85 percent water and easily decompose into humus. In fact, clippings add fertilizer back into the lawn; a 1,000-square-foot lawn can produce almost 400 pounds of grass clippings a year, adding valuable nutrients as it decomposes.

If you insist on raking the lawn, then use the clippings as mulch around shrubs, ornamentals and vegetables, spreading them out over a layer of newspapers. The mulch should be at least an inch thick — 2 to 3 inches won't hurt — to make it work. In the fall the whole concoction can be tilled into the ground, ink and all.

If you want to use chemicals such as 2,4-D to kill broadleaf weeds and didn't get the job done in March, now is a good time to continue the process. You should also be able to use a pre-emergent crab-grass killer in the first two weeks of the month, at least in the cooler northern sections of our area. If you use an herbicide, be sure to wait a few weeks before using those grass clippings as mulch. Herbicide residue can damage some mulched plants.

It may not be a problem yet, but remember that lawns can be severely damaged if you mow during the midday when temperatures are in the mid-90s and the soil is very dry.

Actually, you might be severely damaged during such times too. So wait until the cooler part of the day, or after the lawn has been well-watered.

WATERING THE LAWN — There is nothing more important to grass than regular — and proper — watering. To get downright scientific about it, most Kentuckiana soils can hold 2 to 3 inches of extractable water in the top 4 inches, which is where most of the feeder roots live and play.

Roughly put, that's about 400 gallons of water per 1,000 square feet of landscape. That translates to about an inch of rainfall or irrigation per week, every week, from April through September.

Watering your lawn should never be arbitrary — or capricious. You water with hoses — or a soaker hose — to supplement the God-given moisture from on high, and watering should be done whenever the soil feels dry an inch below the surface, when the leaves begin to wilt or when the grass turns yellowish or blue-green. A general rule of thumb is: If it hasn't rained in a week, it's time to add some water.

There are exceptions to this. A newly planted lawn should be watered daily, even twice daily if you can manage it. Also, in the event of serious heat and drought — when water is being rationed — it's better to allow fescue to go dormant than to underwater it. As several summers in the last few years have proved, dormant grass will recover very nicely, thank you, once the waters begin to fall again. However, this rule doesn't apply to bluegrass lawns, which you don't want to let go dormant; keep watering them.

As with houseplants, overwatering grass can also cause serious problems, including shallow roots, nutrient loss and oxygen deficiency. But more watering is obviously needed during the hotter months, when you are mowing your grass a little extra short to give it that manicured look, or if you have planted certain, less-drought-tolerant varieties, such as Kentucky bluegrass.

Early-morning watering is often more advantageous, but the boss may not buy into the notion that you were two hours late for work because your tall fescue needed a little extra water.

If you're not certain how much water you're dumping on the lawn, just set a rain gauge, coffee can or flat, shallow dish or pie pan under the sprinkler and measure it yourself. Let the water run for a half-hour to see exactly how much falls in that time. Then invest in one of those gadgets that fits over the water spigot and automatically shuts off the water at the right time.

This watering stuff, however, can be very tricky. Large landscape plants will suck up water from nearby turf, and a tree may take two or three times as much water as the grass, so keep those pesky roots in mind while watering.

THAT DARN THATCH — We already know that thatch is mostly layers of organic matter, dead or living, including stems and roots, that develop between the soil and the vegetation. An accumulation of 1/2 to 1 inch of thatch interferes with water and air movement and creates a favorable environment for insects and diseases.

The good news is that a lot of people talk about thatch, but few of us get it. Few of us fertilize and water our lawns to the point where thatch becomes a major problem.

Tall fescue and perennial ryegrass — the lawns of choice around here — never develop enough thatch to be a problem. Bluegrass lawns should be dethatched only in the spring or fall, never in the summer. Zoysia grass should be dethatched in early to mid-summer.

You can rent a spiffy dethatcher machine at most rental or big gardening shops. It's a "vertical" mower that cuts through the thatch down to the soil surface, cutting up the organic matter and depositing it on the surface. If you have a lot of thatch, you might want to crisscross your yard several times. The organic matter cut loose by the machine should be raked up and dumped in the compost pile.

Then go back out to your lawn and just listen to it breath: "Oooooh, aaaaaah, do I feel good, clean and ready to grow!"

GARDEN TIPS
EARLY

If you want to start flowers or warm-season vegetables like tomatoes, peppers and eggplant indoors to get them ready for planting outdoors in May, April 1 is a good day to begin.

Plant the seeds in a container of good, sterile potting soil. After the container has been thoroughly soaked, sprinkle the top of the growing medium with milled sphagnum moss. Often when the little seedlings are breaking through the soil they are hit with a disease called "damping off," but I've never had that happen with a 1/8-inch thick layer of milled sphagnum.

Next, place the container in a clear plastic bag and seal the end, creating a miniature greenhouse. Another trick I use is to place the bag in front of a floor heat register or at the foot of the refrigerator. That will provide enough heat.

If you place the bag in the sun, you might end up with prematurely cooked vegetables. One hazard of placing the bag in front of the refrigerator, however, is that sometimes you end up with depressions that look suspiciously like a dropped package of frozen hot dogs.

Watch the seeds closely. As soon as the tiny plants poke their heads through the soil and begin looking around, place them about three to four inches below a bank of fluorescent lights. Government studies, and my experience, have shown that regular cool, white fluorescent lights are just as effective in starting plants as the more expensive grow lights.

But if you like the distinctive color the grow lights give your plants, try mixing one plain fluorescent tube and one grow light in your white enamel fixture.

Early April is the time to prepare the royal rose, the Queen of Flowers, for another growing season.

First remove the protective mounds of mulch you put around the roses last fall, but don't take it too far away because you may need it again for one of our spring freezes. Also, be careful not to break off some of the new basal shoots that developed beneath the mound of mulch while you were out buying Valentine's Day candy.

Once the mulch has been removed, an application of fertilizer will get the roses off and running. Monty Justice, a member of the Louisville Rose Society, recommends a liquid fertilizer supplement called Watch Us Grow combined with a teaspoon of chelated iron per gallon of water. He pours this over each rose bush at the rate of one gallon for every three square feet. He does this every seven to 10 days until four applications have been made. Be sure to water the ground well before using this treatment.

Another excellent rose gardener who was a very good friend of mine, the late "Uncle Charlie" Dawson of Simpsonville, Ky., recommended applying a tablespoon of Epsom salts per plant in the spring and then repeating the treatment 90 days later. He said this prevents leaf loss. Epsom salts are a very convenient and inexpensive form of magnesium, which helps in the manufacture of chlorophyll, the plant's "green machine."

It's still early April, so there's no big hurry to prune. You can remove the weak or rotted stems, but be sure to toss them in the trash so diseases don't hang around. If you're not sure which shoots to prune, wait another week. When pruning, make the cut at an angle just above the new shoot developing on the outside edge of last year's cane.

If you have just a few roses, you might consider putting a thumb tack in the cut ends of the canes, a trick Uncle Charlie taught me to keep the dreaded borer from sneaking into the tips.

It's also time to begin your spray program of insecticides and fungicides. Extra work now will reward you with a summer rose that would have made Uncle Charlie beam with pride.

Moist early spring weather is favorable for Botrytis blight, or tulip fire disease. The disease may appear on leaves as small gray or tan oval spots having a water-soaked margin. The blight may also produce stunted, distorted and rolled leaves.

Tulip fire disease can destroy a whole tulip bed in just a few days of wet, humid weather. To prevent it, be sure the bed is in an area with good drainage, keep the bed weeded, remove and destroy old flowers and spray, if needed, with fungicides such as Zineb, Ferbam or Maneb.

DO NOT cut back the leaves of healthy plants. Let them die back naturally, because the bulb needs their help to store up food for next year's assault on your senses.

If you don't like the look of a bed full of headless tulips, interplant with summer annuals like geraniums and impatiens.

Carrots can be planted any time in early April, but getting them to germinate in cooler weather can be a problem. One way to jump-start any seeds is to soak them in water for a few hours, which can hurry germination outdoors.

Once outdoors, the biggest spring problem is the continual crusting over of the soil due to rain and baking sun. You can beat this by placing a board over the row or a piece of damp burlap which you can easily keep moist. Just remember to remove these covers as soon as the new seedlings appear, or you may hear muffled cries for help.

Another trick is to plant radish seeds with carrot seeds. The fast germinating radishes will break up the crust, but be sure to remove some of the radishes or the carrots won't have room to grow.

Radishes are best harvested early anyway. If they get too big, they get hot, and the only thing worse than biting into a warm weather radish is gargling with Tabasco sauce.

Now that April is here, it's time to check the tubers and corms of the gladioluses and cannas you stored last fall. You should have sprinkled a little fungicide over them when you stored them. If you spot any rotten ones, throw them away immediately. One bad tuber or corm can ruin a whole barrel of glads or cannas very quickly. Don't plant the good ones yet, however; it's much too early. They need warm weather to get started.

You can start your tuberous begonias inside now. Begin with a good soil mix of one part potting soil, one part perlite and one part organic matter. Plant the tubers in a pot with drainage holes, then tip each tuber slightly so water does not collect in the indented crowns, which must be facing up. Place your begonias in a window receiving bright sunlight to assure good growth.

This is the season for wild garlic, a tufted, obnoxious weed that looks like an onion and definitely smells like one, especially when you trim off the tops with a lawn mower.

Wild garlic can be controlled with 2,4-D weedkiller if it is applied when air temperatures reach 55 to 60 degrees for two or three days. The same chemical can also kill broadleaf weeds such as dandelions and plantain.

Always read the label and apply only as directed. For small patches of wild garlic or dandelions, I use an old plastic sprinkling can marked with a big red "X." That way I can spot-treat the lawn, applying the chemical directly to the problem area rather than spraying the whole lawn.

Since the sprinkling can is marked with a red "X," I know it can never be used for anything else. The residue from 2,4-D weedkiller will linger inside the can, and if it were used to water the garden, it would bring a quick end to the growing season.

If you planted some new trees last fall and wrapped them with protective paper, it's time to remove the wrapping and let the little guys breathe. Never leave any kind of wrap on a tree in warm weather because it is the perfect place for insects and diseases to develop.

If you're thinking about planting a new tree this spring, think about the ultimate size of the tree before you plant. That cute little pin oak planted too close to the house might be taking out your gutters in a few years.

When you decide what tree you want, find a mature specimen of that variety somewhere in your community. Stand with your back against the trunk and walk to the outer drip line, which is the outer reaches of the branches, and write down how many steps you took.

Then put a stake in the ground where you want the tree, and walk the same distance in all directions, putting additional stakes in the ground. Stand back and take a look at the area the tree will eventually occupy.

Trees are among the most valuable additions to the home landscape. They can add hundreds of dollars to the value of property — if they are planted properly.

If you ordered new trees from a catalog, chances are they will arrive bare-rooted. With these trees, or any kind of shrubs, it's best to soak the roots in cool water 24 hours before planting.

Dig the hole about 12 inches deeper and wider than the roots. The old practice was to amend the soil with sand or peat moss, but that is no longer the case. The new theory is that the soil we have here is basically clay, and if you make it nice and loamy like potting soil, the roots become weak as they grow through it. When the roots reach the clay, they are too weak to penetrate it and will grow around the side of the hole, eventually strangling the plant. This is true even if the new tree comes in a burlap ball.

When digging, put the dirt in two piles, with the top six inches in one pile and the rest in another. When planting the tree or shrub, use the top soil to fill in around the roots since it is the best. Fill the hole three-quarters full of soil, tamp gently, then fill with water and let it drain away. Then finish filling the hole, being sure the soil is not above the graft at the base of the tree. Leave a little depression around the base of the tree to catch rainwater.

Anything but burlap must be removed from around the root ball. The burlap will disintegrate. Be sure to water your new tree or shrub every week if Mother Nature does not.

Larger trees should be staked.

Two of the ugliest words to pop up around here in a long time are "dogwood anthracnose." It's a fungal disease that's caused a lot of concern — if not panic — in areas such as ours where a spring without dogwoods is unthinkable.

The disease is very real, killing thousands of trees along the East Coast. It's even been spotted in a few areas of Kentucky. Its telltale signs include leaf spots that are medium to large with purple edges, along with tan or "scorched" places on the leaves. As the disease progresses from the leaves to the lower twigs and branches, cankers will form on the stems.

This should not, however, be confused with the more common spot anthracnose that causes pinhead spots on leaves and even other routine discolorations on the leaves. The point is it takes an expert to identify the disease. If you think you may have it, take a small infected branch to your extension agent for proper diagnosis.

The good news is that the disease seems most prevalent in mountainous areas where moisture and humidity are delivered in low-hanging clouds every day. Landscape trees are not nearly as susceptible to the disease. While researchers are looking for resistant varieties — and the late-blooming kousa dogwood is one — here are a few tips to protect the dogwood:

Don't dig trees from the woods; buy them from reputable nurseries. Plant in an open area where air circulation is good and the tree gets at least some sunshine every day. Water trees well in times of drought. Mulch around the tree. In late fall or winter prune off the suckers or water sprouts, which the disease seems to prefer.

MIDDLE

Mid- to late April is a good time to plant both snap and lima beans provided the soil is warm enough, about 45 degrees. I recommend using a soil thermometer to test the temperature; such thermometers are sold at most large gardening centers.

In addition to having the right temperature, beans can be encouraged to sprout quickly with a 30-minute bath in warm water before hitting the ground;

but if it's been a particularly cool spring, you might as well wait another week, especially with the more sensitive lima beans. Even if they do sprout in cool weather, they might rot before sticking their noses up through the soil.

Also, be sure not to plant the seeds too deep. One inch is plenty. It also helps to mix a little sand with the soil to let the sprouts push up more easily, especially in clay.

Be careful not to overwater because the roots can drown easily. Light applications of fertilizer as a side-dressing will help, but go easy on the nitrogen. Especially hot weather will stop pollen growth and cause bean blossoms to drop, so all you can do is wait for the weather to change.

When it's extremely hot, I recommend using a soaker hose placed at about the drip line of the plants. The drier the foliage, the less likely they will have disease problems.

Most gardeners space rows of bush beans two to three feet apart. But one year, as an experiment, my youngest daughter, Jeneen, planted her beans in a block about 10 feet long and four feet wide with only an inch or two between rows. She had a difficult time getting the weeds out of those narrow rows, but as the beans developed, they shaded out a lot of the weeds. The thick covering also kept the soil much moister than in my patch, where the rows were two to three feet apart.

When all was said and done, her bean block outproduced my bean rows about two to one. However, I would allow a little more room between the rows — at least three inches.

As soon as those spring-flowering shrubs have finished blooming, get out the pruning shears and get busy. Shrubs that bloom in the spring should be pruned as soon as the flowers fade, and before new growth begins.

Plants that bloom before mid-June should be pruned after they are finished blooming. They bloom on old wood, and early spring pruning would eliminate the blossoms.

Plants that bloom after mid-June can be pruned in late winter or early spring because they bloom on new wood — wood that is produced in mid- to late spring.

By pruning, I don't mean shear the tops off. Look down inside the shrubs and select 20 percent of the old, thickest canes and cut them off as close to the ground as you can. The more open the shrub, the better the light can penetrate down inside the shrub, promoting new growth for next year.

Acid-loving azaleas can be pruned after blooming, but only if you really need to keep them in bounds. Azaleas look much better if they are allowed to grow naturally. Spring-flowering shrubs should be fertilized immediately after they finish blooming, and then again one month later.

Also, cut off the faded blossoms on rhododendrons. If you do, you will have many more blossoms the following year.

It is a little early to plant muskmelons and watermelons, but you can get a big jump on the season by buying transplants or starting some on your own. If you purchase them or start them yourself, be sure they are started in individual peat containers so they can be planted without disturbing their roots.

Another trick is to lay sheets of black plastic in your melon patch two to three weeks before planting to warm the soil, then cut slits in the plastic for planting.

Have you checked your strawberries yet? Be sure to remove the winter mulch when you see the strawberries start to grow and before the buds emerge from the crown. Be careful not to break off the sensitive buds. If you're thinking about planting strawberries this spring, be sure to remember to plant them so the dirt comes halfway up the crown.

If you had spittle bugs in your strawberries last year — those are tiny, yellowish-green insects that hide in balls of their own froth — apply Thiodan early. Once strawberries start to ripen, you can't use chemicals to get at the bugs.

If it's been a particularly severe winter, the leaves on your magnolia tree may look as if they've been bronzed for posterity. But remember, this is as far north as you will find the magnolia grandiflora, and such winter damage will occur every time the temperature drops to zero or below.

What to do now? Fertilize them with a fertilizer formulated for magnolias and keep them well-watered during dry periods in spring and summer. Many will come back a lot better than you think.

The pruning of peach trees in the spring should be delayed until just before bloom. To prune a peach tree remove the central leader and leave side limbs that form a little basket, or pinwheel, so sun can reach the center.

Never prune in the fall. Even mid-winter pruning can hasten plant development in the spring, which could be damaged by a late spring freeze. Apples, however, can be pruned as early as late February.

How do you check for fruit-bud damage after a tough winter? Dead buds will not swell in the spring if they are killed in the winter. If injury occurs closer to the time the fruit tree blooms, the flower center, or pistil, will be black.

In the case of apple or pear trees, you can cut across the flower and remove the top half to get a better look at the underlying tissue.

By looking at 25 to 50 buds, or flowers, you can get a rough estimate of injury.

Recent studies have shown that when peach trees reach full bloom, a temperature of 27 degrees will kill about 10 percent of the blossoms, but 24 degrees, just a little drop, will kill 90 percent.

Apple trees in the "full pink" stage will lose 10 percent of the crop at 28 degrees, but 90 percent at 25 degrees.

Tree roots begin absorbing nutrients when the soil temperature goes above 40 degrees, which often occurs in April. New research indicates that a tree's roots will extend well beyond the drip line at its outer edge — a tree 45 feet tall might have roots extending 40 feet beyond the drip line. Keep that in mind when watering and fertilizing.

The old method of boring holes to fertilize trees is no longer popular. Spread granular or liquid fertilizer over the surface of the soil. Feeder roots grow up to just an inch under the soil surface.

LATE

Henry Kirchner, one of the area's best vegetable growers, called me toward the end of April one year to warn me that the aphids had arrived.

Aphids are tiny sucking insects that multiply like ants at a picnic and seem to take over a whole plant overnight. Henry called to say that the aphids were trying to take over his cabbages and that all gardeners should look for them in the spring.

Insecticides like Malathion and Spectracide will help, but so will something else that might surprise you — aluminum foil used as a reflective mulch.

Entomologists at the U.S. Department of Agriculture's Maryland research center said using sheets of aluminum foil as a mulch will repel sucking insects like aphids that transmit viral diseases from plant to plant. The scientists said the use of aluminum foil in muskmelon plots will reduce aphids by 96 percent and also repel leaf hoppers, thrips and Mexican bean beetles.

We are now well into a new growing season, and those tender plants of peas, broccoli, cabbage and cauliflower look tempting to any rabbit in the neighborhood.

Over the years I have tried or looked at almost every method of rabbit control. Most of the methods include applying a chemical to the foliage of the plant. They don't work consistently because one rainfall will wash away all the protection.

One method I did see that worked was the use of small-hole wire called hardware cloth. The gardener made a tent-like structure out of wire as long as his row of peas, with another piece of wire stretched across each end. The tent was about eight inches high, and by the time his peas had grown that big the rabbits had found another feeding ground. The wire could be stored easily in his barn over the winter.

In smaller gardens, gallon-sized milk jugs with their bottoms cut out make perfect protective greenhouses for baby broccoli, cabbage and cauliflower plants. They will keep out the rabbits, marauding birds looking for nesting material, and — with their caps screwed on — provide frost-free homes on frosty spring mornings.

These early plants can go outdoors as soon as the ground can be worked, but frost-free protection is important because cauliflower will have a hard time recuperating from temperatures below 25 degrees, and too much cold can force broccoli to form scattered heads instead of one nice big one, but that often depends on the health of the transplants.

When the heads of cauliflower get two to three inches wide, you can tie the tops of the leaves over the developing heads or the sun will turn them a pinkish or purplish color, and they will not be good to eat. The leaves can be tied with twine or even clipped together with big wooden clothespins.

But I think the best way to "blanch" the crop is to tuck a wadded-up piece of aluminum foil inside the leaves. It will keep the light out and allow for better air circulation.

People ask me dozens of times every spring which is the best insecticide to use to get the ants off the peonies. The answer is none.

Peony buds have a sugar coating on them, and all the ants are doing is loading up on calories, not harming the plant. In fact, I've read that the sticky coating could prevent the peony buds from opening if the ants weren't there, so leave them alone.

One other thought about peonies: If you look closely at each stem, you will see one large bud at the tip end and smaller buds forming along the stem in the back. Remove the smaller buds. Leave only the large bud. You will have a much better flower display.

I'm often asked why peonies fail to bloom. Often the reason is lack of sun or competition from the roots of nearby shrubs or trees. But the prime reason is because they were planted too deep. The eyes — or buds — of the roots should be no deeper than two inches below the soil. If they get any deeper, you'll never "see" them.

You may notice that some of your evergreen needles are brown or discolored at the tip, or along the margins. The browning is due to desiccation, the loss of moisture from the needles when the ground is frozen and no moisture can be taken from the soil.

April is a good time to fertilize evergreens to help repair the damage. Most evergreens like an "acid-type" fertilizer. The big exception is the taxus, or yew, which does not like acid soil and will be happy with a 10-10-10 fertilizer. That is why you shouldn't plant taxus around acid-loving azaleas or rhododendrons.

You may also notice cracked and split bark on your deciduous trees as a result of the bark freezing at night and thawing in the day. We used to use wound dressings to try to heal these splits, but research indicates that the dressings can do more harm than good. About all you can do is let Mother Nature run her course.

April is a time when you see tent

caterpillars crawling into the crotches of cherry and crab-apple trees. Their large white tents can be eliminated with Sevin, Malathion or Spectracide, although a better idea is to use biologically safe Dipel or Thuricide, i.e., bacillus thuringensis, which is totally safe to man.

If you do not want to use any chemicals, prune away the whole branch, drop it in a can and burn it. Either way, only attack the critters close to sundown when they've gone home to the tent after a day of foraging.

FRED'S TIPS

Here's one idea I got from a couple of listeners for getting crops like carrots and beets off to a great start in the spring: Instead of planting them at ground level, plant them in a ridge.

The trick is to take the hoe and work the soil into a ridge about three inches high. Then make a furrow along the ridge about 1/4 inch deep. Plant the seeds in the furrow, covering them with either rotted sawdust or peat moss. Wet the material and keep it damp until the seeds germinate.

I think this method is good because it allows the roots of the carrots and beets to expand in the soil, and the soil cannot become firm or crusty.

Another helpful hint is to place a wide board over the row. Elevate the board an inch or so by supporting it with bricks. That shades the soil, allows it to stay damp, and it's easier for seeds to germinate.

DO NOT apply Sevin during the bloom period of any of your orchard crops because pesticides are toxic to bees. Bees that aren't killed by direct contact in the orchard often carry the pesticide back to the hive, where it may kill the brood.

Over-mulching can be as dangerous to your crops as running a steamroller through the cabbage patch. It is especially dangerous to shallow-rooted beauties such as azaleas, rhododendrons, dogwoods, boxwoods, hollies and many trees. If you keep adding mulch every year — and some people will pile it up 10 to 12 inches deep — it will suffocate the plant. It will also lead to disease. Two to three inches of mulch is plenty.

People ask me every year what kind of fertilizer to use in the garden. The best answer is to test your soil through your county extension office. It's the only way to determine exactly what you will need to produce healthy vegetables, flowers, shrubs and trees.

But if you did not do that last fall and time is running short, I would recommend that you apply 25 pounds of 5-10-10 or 6-12-12 fertilizer per 1,000 square feet of gardening area. If you plan to grow Sugar Anne snap peas in containers on the patio, add two tablespoons of 5-10-10 or 6-12-12 per bushel of soil.

For better beans, don't plant them in the same space two years in a row. Some diseases will linger in the soil from year to year, causing problems. You can also dust the seeds and the soil bed with a fungicide.

If you were lucky enough to get a lily for Easter, here's how to take care of it:

Easter lilies need bright, indirect light, not full sun. The soil in the pot should be slightly damp but not soggy. Poke a hole through the decorative foil or remove it completely so the lilies don't get water-soaked toes.

Pick off the yellow tips of the anthers (with tweezers) before they shed their messy pollen. Rotate the pot a quarter turn each day so the lilies will grow straight and not toward the sun.

After the flowers have faded, set the plant outside in full sun. In a week or two, when the plant is acclimated to the outdoors, take it from the pot and put it in a sunny spot in the garden. It may bloom again late the same year, but chances are it will wait and bloom again the following year and last many more years in your garden.

Gardeners often call me in April wondering why their rhubarb develops seed stalks so early in the season. The answer is low fertility in the garden. Rhubarb should be fertilized in early spring with good, all-purpose vegetable garden fertilizer. Be sure to remove the seed stalks that develop this time of year. Don't let the plant go to seed because that will be the end of the crop.

If you lost a landscape tree this past winter and are thinking of replacing it, do not fall for ads about super fast-growing trees. Trees that grow fast usually grow brittle and weak and are often the first to come down in summer windstorms.

If you buy a plant in a container, take a look at the root system as you remove it. If the roots are all matted, take a very sharp knife and cut through them much like you score a ham before putting it in the oven. This will open up the roots and allow them to grow out into the soil instead of in a circle around the rootball.

Here are a few tips for keeping your lovely lilacs, the Perfume Bottles of Spring, healthy and fragrant.

French lilacs, which are now the most popular, should be allowed to grow at least eight feet tall before being thinned out. Cut out a few of the larger stems at ground level to encourage new shoots, and, of course, remove all dead shoots.

The thinning should be done right after they flower, or in winter. A mature French lilac should be 12 to 15 feet tall. Korean lilacs are only 4 to 8 feet tall at maturity.

About the only insect to affect lilacs are stem borers that invade old wood. This is another reason to prune out old, dead wood.

If you want to prune the top to shape

the lilac bush, do it right after the spring flowering. Next spring's flowers will develop this summer, and if you wait until fall, you'll chop them off. Be sure to fertilize right after the flowering to encourage new buds. Use a balanced fertilizer, like 10-10-10.

It's best to plant or transplant lilacs in the fall, although spring will work with good care and watering. Plant them in full sun in an area that gets good circulation. That will help cut down mildew in the fall. So will sprays of Benlate during the summer.

If an old bush is slowly being taken over by the shadows and roots of a growing tree, dig up the bush, divide the pieces, and get it back in the sun. It may take a few years to bloom again, but it will be worth it.

FRED'S SUPER TIP

If cold, wet spring weather prevented you from getting some of your favorite early spring vegetable seeds sown, don't fret. I've got a suggestion on how you can make up for the lost time: Soak your seeds before you plant them.

Soaking seeds in water prior to planting them is not new.

American Indians filled shallow clay dishes with sand and planted bean seeds in them. The planted dishes were covered with warm ashes for three or four days to speed up germination. As soon as roots began to develop, the beans were dropped into holes in the garden and covered with soil. This procedure was mostly used for planting early crops when the cool soil would tend to rot seeds planted in the usual manner.

Modern-day presoaking is simple. It requires only a small plastic bag, preferably one with a "zipper-lock"-type closing, (shredded) sphagnum moss, or a wet paper towel.

First, let me explain the moss. This is not peat moss. Shredded moss is the long, ropy moss — available at most large garden centers — that is used for lining hanging baskets. This moss contains a natural chemical defense against diseases that can kill seeds as they sprout. Ordinary peat moss should not be used because it does not have this disease-inhibiting agent.

When you open the bag you will find the shredded moss to be as dry as desert sand. You must moisten it before you use it. To do this, roll up a handful of moss in a damp paper towel. Wet the towel again and squeeze the excess moisture out of it.

What you are doing is forcing water into the moss. Repeat the process several times until the moss is thoroughly wet. Then let the towel sit about an hour.

Mark the plastic bag with the seed variety and the date. Tape the front of the seed package to the bag. Put the wet moss in the bag and pour the seeds into the moss. Seal the bag and place it in a warm, light area. Do not use a sunny window. Light is not all that important to germination, and you could cook the seeds if the bag is placed in full sun. I like to put the bag at the foot of our refrigerator. The warm air that circulates there is perfect for this process.

While this is the best way to presprout

your seeds, there is a shortcut I have
successfully used on occasions. In place
of the moss, wet a paper towel and
pour the seeds into it. Then put the wet
towel in the plastic bag. This will work,
but you do not have the natural
defense against seed-killing diseases
that you have with the shredded moss.

Be ready to plant the sprouted seeds
when about half the seeds have pushed
out roots or shoots. If rain delays planting, slow down the process by placing
the bag in a cooler location.

When planting the sprouted seeds
outdoors, do it quickly. Have the soil
all worked and the furrow made before
you open the bag. Sprouts can be killed
by exposure to wind or sunlight.

Don't worry about sprouted seeds
being placed upside down or sideways
in the furrow. They will straighten
themselves out in the sunlight.

May

▣ May Checklist

LAWN TIPS

☐ Examine your lawn for diseases and insect damage.
☐ Mow and water . . . mow and water . . . mow and water.
☐ Hand-pick noxious weeds or apply broadleaf herbicides.

EARLY

☐ Check holly trees for leaf miner.
☐ Prune evergreens.
☐ Take steps to prevent bacterial wilt of cucumbers and melon crops.
☐ Prune rhododendrons.
☐ Move houseplants outdoors.
☐ Repot and fertilize indoor plants.
☐ Buy and plant seedlings for bedding plants.
☐ Plant luffa gourd seeds.

MIDDLE

☐ Check cedar trees for cedar-apple rust gall.
☐ Plant corn in blocks.
☐ Check maple trees for maple petiole borers and wart-like galls.
☐ Check magnolia trees for weevils.
☐ Set out pepper plants when warm enough.
☐ Thin bedding flowers, beets, carrots, loosehead lettuce, onions, radishes and spinach.
☐ Check hanging plants for whiteflies and proper moisture.
☐ Remove faded flowers from peonies.

LATE

☐ Pick strawberries.
☐ Divide irises and check for iris borer.
☐ Plant gladioluses.
☐ Thin fruit on apple, pear and peach trees.
☐ Check dogwood trees for borers.
☐ Check roses for "wild growth."
☐ Check evergreens and trees for bagworms.

SUPER TIP

☐ Raising super tomatoes.

May is the month when the flowers are starting to take shape; there's already fresh lettuce, spinach and radishes on the kitchen table, and the awful heat of summer is still on the horizon — right next to the thunderstorms.

May is named for Maia, the Roman goddess of spring and growth, who was probably eight feet tall by her 16th birthday.

The average high temperature for May is 76.2 degrees, the average low is 54.6 degrees, which means you can now get those tomatoes and peppers out into the garden — the pansies.

Average rainfall in May is 4.15 inches. By the end of a "normal" May — if there is such a thing — you should have an accumulation of 19.60 inches of precipitation, about half the average annual total of 43.56 inches.

The rainiest May in history occurred in 1983, when 10.58 inches fell. The driest was 1932, when only .63 inches of rain fell, which is about the era of the Western "Dust Bowl."

The warmest May date in history was May 28, 1911, when the temperature hit 98 degrees. The coldest, speaking of late frosts, was 31 degrees. It happened twice, on May 1, 1963, and May 10, 1966.

The truly awful news is that 1 inch of snow fell in Louisville on May 6, 1898, which was the latest snowfall in history.

There are 13 hours and 47 minutes of sun on May 1, and 14 hours and 37 minutes of sun on May 31. The average soil temperature ranges from 65 to 75 degrees.

May 6, 1856, was the birth date of Sigmund Freud, the founder of psychoanalysis and a man who, if he were alive today, would say we're all nuts to spend so much time in the garden.

LAWN TIPS

Now that May has arrived, your tomatoes have been planted, and the entire yard has begun to shine in earnest. So it's time to examine one of the three biggest enemies of your lawn: disease.

The good news is that disease ranks third in lawn-care problems, well behind weeds and insects. The bad news is that disease will occasionally sneak in, especially in weather that is abnormally hot or cold.

The most important thing to remember is that having a well-watered, well-fertilized lawn will prevent most diseases before they even get a start, and fall is the best time to fertilize. Disease-causing organisms are always present in your lawn, ready to infect the weakened plants when conditions become favorable. But healthy lawns seldom have disease problems.

Not all the unsightly brown or gray patches you see on your lawn are the result of disease. A lack of water, excess moisture, fertilizer scorch, animal excretions, mechanical damage or even insects living beneath the surface — those dreaded grubs are a classic example — can leave the appearance of disease. However grubs do little damage in the spring so ignore them. They are lazy now — getting ready to become "big boys" — brown beetles that drive you crazy on a lighted patio on a warm spring night, flying with "thunks" against the screen. Even differences in soil in your yard can create a different look in your lawn.

Several fungi diseases are actually common in lawns, but are not necessarily dangerous. In fact, University of Kentucky experts discourage the use of any fungicides on the home lawn because lawns tend to recover on their own. Applying fungicides may cause more problems than the disease.

Also, remember this: Applications of fungicide on lawns that already have patches of brown, gray or injured grasses will not bring those sick areas back to life; fungicides must be applied before the disease hits to do any good.

The conditions that caused the disease often may have disappeared before the fungus is noticed. But it doesn't hurt to make regular trips around the lawn looking for trouble or to keep a sharp eye out for disease while mowing. An unchecked disease can do enormous damage, as many golf course superintendents can testify.

The general rule is that if your lawn has a disease problem that looks more serious than you can deal with, please, please, call in professional advice.

If you must apply fungicides yourself, remember that, as with almost everything else in life, timing is everything. The tough part is applying the fungicide just as heat and humidity conspire to do the most damage to your lawn. Some systemic fungicides are absorbed by the grass and work within the grass plants. Others are active on the leaf surface, but can be washed away by rain. In general, granular applications are applied to the grass when it is wet with dew, or must be washed in, and often are not as effective.

If you are more interested in organic treatments, remember that careful mowing and watering are two keys to keeping a lawn happy.

To that point, a University of Kentucky lawn expert, Paul C. Vincelli, has almost reluctantly concluded that there is no evidence that "biocontrol" of lawn diseases — covering the lawn with "organic" compost-amended top dressings — do any good. In fact top dressings applied on a weekly basis may do more harm than good since compost contains soluble nitrogen, and high nitrogen fertility enhances some diseases such a brown patch.

Keeping that in mind, here are some diseases to watch for:

BROWN PATCH — Brown patch is a series of large, generally oval to round blemishes that often develop during hot, humid, rainy weather. They may be as large as 3 to 10 feet in diameter, often with a black ring of spores at their outer edge. They are often found in tall fescue, perennial ryegrass and some Kentucky bluegrass. Dead leaves tend to remain erect.

Brown patch is one of our most serious problems, often developing on intensively managed lawns that have received excessive nitrogen fertilization and excessive irrigation.

Lawns in areas with bad air circulation often suffer the most from brown patch. Thin out trees or shrubs with very selective pruning to allow more circulation. In most cases, brown spot can be treated with good lawn practices. Fungicides are needed only in very serious cases, in which case you may have to till the ground and reseed in the fall.

COTTONY BLIGHT — Another disease that comes with hot, humid weather is cottony blight. It is often seen early in the morning as masses of cottonlike growth within the lawn, leaving blades that appear streaked and water-soaked.

Poor soil drainage is often the cause; the disease will follow the outline of any wet spots in your lawn. Too much nitrogen fertilizer and poor air circulation are also contributors.

DOLLAR SPOT — Dollar spot is a series of silver-dollar-sized brown or whitish-tan spots in the lawn, especially in bluegrass, which is a cool-weather grass. Two fungi cause the disease, one in cool weather and the other in warm weather. Either one is most likely to occur during dry soil conditions, so be sure your lawn gets adequate moisture.

The disease is most prevalent where dew hangs longest in the mornings, and you may see tufts of a whitish fungus on some blades.

FAIRY RING — An interesting, almost fun thing to find on your lawn, a fairy ring is a ring of toadstools that develop in a circular pattern in the grass, often accompanied by a circle of dark-green grass.

The toadstools are almost always caused by dead or decaying tree roots in the ground, especially in hot, wet weather. The fungi do not infect the lawn grasses but can build up enough vegetative matter to choke out the grass. Just sweep up the toadstools with a rake and throw them away. Good fall fertilization will bring back the grass.

FUSARIUM BLIGHT — Fusarium blight often accompanies the "dog days" of summer, from late June until September. It's most damaging where a thick thatch has been allowed to form above the lawn surface. It causes tan blotches somewhat similar to brown patch, but with fusarium wilt some green grass is often left in the patch, giving it a "frog eye" look — darker in the center than at the edges.

RED THREAD — If you see bright pink to red strands in the grass, especially in the morning when it is wet with dew, you've got red thread. These patches will often be 6 to 12 inches wide. It mostly occurs in times of moderate temperature but high humidity. Ground that is nitrogen-deficient is the best incubation place for it.

SLIME MOLD — Sometimes when hot, humid weather hits suddenly you will notice a mass of light to violet-blue fungi on a clump of grass or several clumps of grass. This is slime mold or "smoke ring." It looks terrible but can easily be brushed away with a broom or rake, or, ironically, washed away with a hose. It will not harm your grass.

SMOKE RING — During times of high humidity and high temperatures, a sparse, grayish fungal growth called a "smoke ring" often appears on newly infected grass in early mornings. It is most apparent on low-cut turf, but disappears quickly as the dew dries off the grass. It causes no permanent damage.

LAWN THINGS TO DO IN MAY:

Water your lawn deeply if you go seven to 10 days without rain.

Keep lawn-mower blade at 2 1/2 inches and make sure it stays sharp; hot weather is coming, and a scalped lawn is susceptible to disease and scorching.

Check for insect damage and disease.

Hand-pick noxious weeds or apply broadleaf herbicides, carefully following directions.

GARDEN TIPS
EARLY

Often, in the first weeks of May, homeowners complain that the leaves of their holly trees are turning yellow and falling off, and they fear the trees are dying. That is rarely the case. This is the time of year when holly trees normally shed their leaves and develop new ones. Take a close look at your "sick-looking holly," and you should see new leaves developing among the stems.

What you should look for on the fallen leaves are signs of the dreaded leaf miner. If the old leaves have what look like gray tunnels or squiggly lines through them, that's a sure sign they are infected with the leaf miner or leaf maggot.

Look for a tiny black fly darting among the newly unfolding leaves. It's laying the eggs that produce the leaf miner. If you see the fly, apply Malathion. If the black flies haven't found your trees yet but the evidence of leaf miner is there from last year's leaves, then I'd apply a systemic insect control like Cygon or Orthene. Whatever you do, be sure to read the label thoroughly and apply only as directed.

Early to mid-May is often the best time to prune conifers — the cone-bearing evergreens such as pines, spruce and firs. These trees produce their yearly growth in one spurt, the light green bursts at the tips of the limbs that we call "candles." This often occurs in early May but could be much earlier during a warm spring.

If you want to shape your tree so it will develop compact, dense growth, prune off the tips of the candles. That will force the tree to develop new shoots below the cut.

Conifers should only be pruned on their candles. If you cut off old growth, it will not regenerate, and your tree can look ugly, if not partially undressed.

It is all right to remove dead or severely damaged limbs close to the trunk, but give that damaged limb a chance to regain its strength before doing anything drastic.

Although your cucumber and muskmelon crops may seem too young and tender to have to worry about "bacterial wilt," now is the time to begin taking measures to prevent it.

Bacterial wilt is the disease that suddenly attacks what appear to be healthy cucumber or melon crops, killing the plants in just a few days. When you cut through the stem of an infected plant, a bead of cloudy, sticky sap can be squeezed from the cut ends. Yuck!

By the time you notice the disease, it's too late to control it. Cucumber beetles, both striped and spotted, have already attacked. They damage the plants by feeding on the leaves, then finish them off with the bacteria they leave behind.

You must begin control early, when seedlings first push up through the ground or the transplants are set. You can use Sevin, diazinon or Rotenone. Spray regularly through the growing season and be sure to spray the undersides of the foliage as well; cucumber beetles can be very sneaky.

Have you pruned those rhododendrons yet? Do it AFTER the flowers have faded. Remove old flowers at their base — just above the point where the new, small green leaves are developing.

If you're pruning to shape the bush, cut as close as possible above a fork or cluster of leaves. Do not leave a long, bare stub. Rhododendrons with long, scraggly stems can be pruned back severely, but the plants may not have many flowers the next season. In following years, the flowers will be more abundant.

In general, however, it's not good to prune back more than one-third of the total number of branches each season. Also, most named varieties of rhododendron are grafted. Cut off any sprouts below the graft because they will not produce the right kind of flowers.

Did you ever fall asleep by the pool, only to wake up feeling as if you'd been scorched to a crisp? Well, houseplants moved outside for the summer — and it's time to think about that — can get a bad case of sunburn too.

Many houseplants, especially those native to the tropics, like the outdoors in the summer. They are used to warm, humid air. We may like air-conditioning in the summer, but when is the last time you saw an air-conditioned nursery or arboretum?

Place your houseplants outdoors in the shade of a nearby tree or tuck them in an outdoor corner where they get all the benefits of humid air and gentle rain but are sheltered from the scorching rays of the sun.

You will have to water more carefully, especially if the plants are in clay pots, because the winds will dry them out more quickly. Also, be sure there is good air circulation around the plants. That will reduce insect and disease problems.

Remember one thing: Your houseplants' outdoor vacation must end when nighttime temperatures fall to about 55 to 60 degrees, which can happen by mid-September.

Every year I get calls from people who ask what they can do to revive houseplants after a cold night outside. Many times the answer is to arrange a decent funeral. Temperatures below 50 degrees can kill many houseplants overnight.

This is a good time of year to repot indoor plants. First, check the bottom of the pots to see if any roots are showing through the drain holes. If they are, you know most of the soil in the pot is full of roots.

For best growth, the plant should be moved to a pot one size larger. Spread some newspapers over a large work area, knock the rootball out of the pot and place it in a larger pot to which you have added drainage material such as small rocks. Then sift a loose potting soil around the rootball, tamping with your fingers as you fill.

Don't cover the rootball any deeper than it was in its former home. Water well and place in a low-light area for a few days, then return it to its regular place at the window. Wait several weeks before applying plant food. Remember, indoor plants should only be fertilized in the spring and summer, the times they are most active.

What should you do with spring-flowering bulbs after they are finished blooming? You already know to let the foliage die back naturally. Never cut away foliage while it is still green. It's producing food for next year's crop.

If you had problems with animals digging up your bulbs over the winter, put chicken wire over the bulb bed when you plant in the fall. It will prevent anything from digging up your bulbs while allowing enough space for the bulbs to grow.

Every weekend now the nurseries and garden centers will be thick with people buying bedding plants, both flowers and vegetables. Treat these annuals like a carton of ice cream; make them your last purchase before heading home.

Once home, protect the seedlings in a shady spot and water well. They must NEVER dry out. When you finally remove the seedling from its plastic cell pack, don't tug from the top. Push the rootball out by pressing on the bottom and sides of the individual cell.

If the bedding plants are sold in one big tray, take a sharp knife and divide the plants as if you were dividing a pan of brownies. If a knife isn't handy, remove all the seedlings and gently tease individual plants apart with your fingers, trying to keep the rootball intact.

Pop your plants into the garden as quickly as possible. If you must plant on a sunny day, wait until late afternoon and mist and water the plants thoroughly as you plant. A very diluted solution of water-soluble fertilizer will help.

It helps to shade the seedlings for three to five days with strawberry baskets, cardboard or a board elevated on bricks. One inventive gardener I know collects old umbrellas and uses them as sunshades. It looks strange, but it works.

For a little gardening fun, consider planting seeds for luffa gourds, which can be used as sponges after they mature.

Most of us have tough places around the home where we would like to grow flowers, but it always seems too hot, dry or exposed in those areas for anything to do well.

There is hope. The National Garden Bureau just released a list of 19 annuals and perennials that will do well, even in a tough, torturous summer.

Here they are, in alphabetical order, the toughest flowers around:

FIBEROUS ROOTED BEGONIAS — These are often those bright, waxy-red flowers you see massed along sidewalks and the entrances to subdivisions. Once established, they need less water than most flowers. They are also reliable bloomers in partial shade. They also come in pink and white.

BUTTERFLY WEEDS — These tall, orange blooms are very attractive to butterflies. They also make great cut flowers.

CELOSIA, or cockscomb — These feathery, plume-like flowers are very attractive later in the summer when not much else wants to bloom. For best performance, grow them from seed, or plant the green plants. They come in red to cream to yellow and are from 4 inches to 4 feet tall.

CLEOME, or spider plants — These leggy beauties thrive on hot, dry conditions and can reach up to 6 feet tall. Their name comes from the distinctive, spider-like growth. They come in violet, rose and white.

COREOPSIS, or pot of gold — Native to North America, the daisy-like flowers come in yellow or red.

COSMOS — A native of Mexico, which should tell you something about heat tolerance, it prefers infertile, but well-drained soil. It comes in scarlet, pink, rose and white.

GLOBE AMARANTH, or gomphrena — This is a tropical native that will last a long time. It has dwarf varieties as well as those that will grow a few feet. It comes in lavender, rose and pink.

MALAMPODIUM — An underused annual with lush green growth and small, yellow, daisy-like flowers in profusion. Often seeds itself from year to year. A real star at the Kentucky State Fair.

MORNING GLORY — This old favorite is best grown from seed and needs some sort of trellis or vertical support because it can grow to 10 feet or more. The flowers are white, blue, pink and red.

NICOTIANA, or flowering tobacco — This tough plant has great bursts of tubular flowers above lush green foliage. It ranges in height from bushy bedding plants to 6 feet. The colors are pink, rose and white.

NIEREMBERGIA — The "Mount Blanc" is the first white-flowering nierembergia grown from seed. Its abundant, pure-white, star-shaped blooms are heat- and insect-tolerant. Its low-growing habit makes it good for rock gardens. A 1991 All America selection.

PETUNIAS — Another old favorite, plant breeders are now working on varieties that bloom longer with less work plucking off all the old buds. Once established they handle drought well. They come in about 250,000 colors and varieties.

PORTULACA, or moss rose — Among the most drought-tolerant of all, the moss rose has distinct, fleshy leaves and comes in cream, red, scarlet, pink and fuchsia. The newer varieties stay open longer in the day and on cloudy days.

SALVIA — Another plant that tolerates heat and drought, blooming prolifically in full-sun gardens. The blue varieties make nice cut flowers. If cut back in late summer it often rewards with a fresh burst of color in the fall.

SUNFLOWERS — The newer varieties of this old favorite are white, bronze and cream as well as yellow. It tolerates heat and poor soil and can zoom to 12 feet in great soil.

VERBENA — The new "Imagination" flower is an intense blue-magenta with fine foliage and rapid plant growth. It's great in the garden or in hanging baskets. It's a 1993 All America selection.

VINCA, or periwinkle — A nice ground cover, this annual is getting more popular all the time. It's usually a low-maintenance high performer found in many shades of white, pink and crimson.

YARROW, or achillea — They are so tough they may need to be controlled in close quarters. Tall and spiky -- or low and profuse -- they come in many shades of yellow, pink and crimson. A great perennial for tough areas.

ZINNIA — Another old favorite, and a bright, prolific Mexican native, zinnias are easily grown from seed into dozens of sizes and colors. The newer varieties are not as prone to mildew as the older varieties. Anyone can grow zinnias successfully.

MIDDLE

If you see an orangish, jellylike mass growing on the branches of your cedar tree, chances are it's cedar-apple rust gall. The galls, ranging from one to two inches in diameter, will keep growing until they fall off the tree. If you have apple trees nearby, remove the galls by hand and destroy them. Do not plant apple trees anywhere near cedar trees because spores from the gall are carried by the wind to the apple trees, infecting the leaves and fruits.

Your baby sprouts of sweet corn will never develop into succulent ears of corn unless you plant the corn in blocks, not one or two long rows.

That's because the corn silks that grow out of the top of the ear — each is attached to one individual kernel on the cob — most be pollinated by the pollen produced by the tassels at the top of the cornstalk. If you plant the corn in one or two straight rows, the wind is liable to blow the pollen the other direction, resulting in poor pollination.

So if you're planting as few as 12 stalks of corn, plant them in three rows with four stalks per row. The same concept holds true if you are planting 120 stalks.

Corn likes a high-nitrogen fertilizer when it is planted and again when it is knee-high. As the ears develop, the corn earworm can be a pest, but it is easily controlled with Sevin.

May is not a time of year normally associated with falling maple leaves, but it can be when the maple petiole borer is at work. The borer has a definite life cycle. The adult female saw-fly emerges in May and lays eggs on the stems of the leaves. When the eggs hatch, yellow, wormlike larvae emerge and begin tunneling into the leaf stalk. As the worm matures, it eats most of the inside of the stem and — pfffft! — the leaf is blown off the tree by the wind.

The worms remain inside the stem. Later on, when the stem falls to the earth, the worms bore into the ground, lay eggs for the sawfly, and the cycle is complete.

What can you do about it? Nothing. The tree damage is minimal. There are still plenty of leaves left for the autumn drop.

Maple leaves are also susceptible to small, wartlike galls that come in a variety of shapes and colors, including red, green and black.

The cause is a mite that spends the winter in the bark of the tree, then moves to the leaves in the spring to feed. As the mites feed on the underside of the leaves, the leaves produce pouchlike galls enclosing the mites. As with the maple petiole borer, they do not cause enough damage to worry about, especially if the tree is fertilized on scheduled.

The large, glossy, evergreen leaves of Southern magnolias are also susceptible to insect problems in the spring. Around here the culprit is generally the night-feeding sassafras weevil, also called the yellow poplar weevil or the magnolia leaf miner.

The adult weevil survives the winter in the leaf litter below the tree. Then, in its beetle stage, it flies to the trees to feed on buds and developing leaves. It will produce big holes in the leaves as well as brown blotches near the leaf tip.

Sevin is the best control. In spraying the tree I would add a drop or two of liquid soap, which helps the spray stick to the glossy surface. Or you can buy what is called "spreader sticker" at garden centers, a special substance that holds the pesticide to the leaves.

Sweet or pungent, long or blocky, hot or mild, the pepper is often the pickiest plant in the spring vegetable patch. That's because peppers do not like cool weather. Do not set them out until night temperatures have risen well above 55 degrees, which can be well into the month of May. Planting peppers too early often results in stunted plants and poor yields.

You can get peppers off on the road to success with a high-phosphorous starter fertilizer such as 8-24-8. Do not give them any additional fertilizer until a good fruit set has developed. You must harvest the fruit regularly so new fruit will set and always rotate tomatoes, eggplant and pepper crops, making sure they do not follow each other in the same location. They are all susceptible to the same soil-borne diseases.

You may feel like Jack the Ripper, but when it comes to gardens, thinning plants is very important to their growth.

It's not an easy thing to do. You have just spent weeks worrying about every one of them, and now you're being asked to rip many of them out.

It must be done. With many plants — and carrots and turnips come quickly to mind — the biggest reason they "go to tops" is because they were not thinned out properly when they were little. They didn't have sufficient space to grow healthy bottoms. In cases such as large-flowering zinnias and marigolds, it helps prevent them from growing into weak-kneed skyscrapers that are easily toppled in summer rainstorms.

You should consider all bedding flowers, as well as beets, carrots, loose-leaf lettuce, onions, radishes and spinach, as candidates for thinning. Pick a time when the ground is damp and soft but not muddy. If the ground has been dry, you should water for an hour beforehand.

Look at the seed package to find the recommended spacing for each variety or check the accompanying vegetable-planting guide. As a rule you can start thinning when your plants have one or two pairs of true leaves — not counting the "seed leaves," which emerge first. Onions should be thinned when they are three to four inches tall.

Gently pull out the unwanted plants without disturbing those that remain. If the remaining plants are disturbed, firm the soil around them, or if the stand is very thick, cut the tops off with scissors, leaving the roots of the neighboring plants undisturbed.

Evening is the best time to thin because the plants will have the cool night to recover.

You can thin vegetables in several stages until the remaining plants are the right distance apart, using the thinnings for taste treats. Many of the flowers you thin, and a few of the vegetables, may be transplanted to other parts of the garden or shared with neighbors. But root crops such as beets, carrots and radishes may develop malformed roots and do not transplant well.

Mid-May is a time when most people find it difficult to resist buying hanging baskets, giving little thought to how much care they will need in the hotter months of June and July.

Fuchsia, for example, are big sellers in the spring but are often dead by July because they can't handle direct sun; they need only a little bit of filtered light in the morning.

Don't ever let the soil of a hanging plant go completely dry. Mist daily and watch for white flies, which dearly love fuchsia. Hanging baskets need pots 10 to 12 inches in diameter, preferably ones made of plastic because they will hold water longer. Use a peatlike potting mix for the best growth and be sure the plants have excellent drainage.

If the leaves of a few of your vegetables, especially potatoes or radishes, are beginning to look as if they were shot full of holes, the likely culprit is the flea beetle. The flea beetle is a very tiny black, brown or metallic-blue bug that often emerges in May.

Its enlarged hind legs enable it to jump like a flea when disturbed. Control is very important because the flea beetles' tiny white larvae feed on roots and seldom can be seen under-ground. The adults, of course, feed above ground, filling the leaves with tiny holes. Fortunately, Sevin and diazinon will control them.

Be sure to remove the faded flowers from your peonies now. If you let the old blossoms go to seed, they will sap the strength from next year's crop. But don't move peonies now unless it's an emergency. The best time to replant, divide or establish new varieties is in late September or October.

LATE

You should be out picking strawberries, if you haven't already been out in the patch sneaking a few of the early ones. And like everything else in life, there is a right way and a wrong way to harvest berries.

Plan A, of course, is to grasp the stem between the forefinger and thumbnail just above the berry. Pull with a slight twisting motion. When the stem breaks, let the berry roll into the palm of your hand. When you have three or four berries in your hand, carefully place the berries in a container. Don't overfill — strawberries stacked over five inches deep will mash the fruit on the bottom.

That's Plan A. University of Kentucky extension specialist Jerry Brown suggests another way to harvest berries: Eat them immediately after picking, and you'll never have to worry about bruises.

After the irises have finished blooming, usually in late May or early June, is the best time to dig and divide them. When you dig a clump you will find many new plants off the sides of the original rhizome. Carefully remove the new plants. But before discarding the old ones, check to see if the roots are riddled with holes, sometimes to the point where they're almost hollow. If they are, the iris borer has paid a visit.

The moth of the adult borer flies at night, laying eggs in fall that will hatch into larvae in the spring. The larvae can be killed with weekly applications of Sevin or Malathion, if they are used from the time growth begins until the end of May. Older larvae can be killed with a systemic insecticide like Cygon. The borer is the iris's biggest enemy, mostly because it introduces a bacteria that causes a soft rot.

Remember when replanting healthy irises to leave the very top of their root sticking out of the soil, much like ducks in water. Don't trim off the leaves; they provide nourishment.

May is a good time to plant gladioluses. With a little planning, you can have these versatile flowers blooming all summer and fall.

Glads, which produce large, showy blossoms along a long, pointed stalk, get their name from "gladius," the Latin word for sword. There is no other cut flower that offers the reds, pinks, yellows, whites, purples and lavenders it produces.

Glads are grown from corms, sensitive, bulblike structures that must be dug up every fall and replanted every spring. Depending on the cultivar, glads take from 60 to 120 days to produce flowers that will bloom for two weeks. Some of the taller varieties need staking to keep from falling over under the weight of their own blooms.

Glad bulbs will open at the bottom of the spike. Cut the flowers after at least three florets have opened. As the lower florets fade, the rest will open. Allow as many leaves as possible to remain on the plant so it will store food for next year.

Now is a good time to thin out the developing fruit on apple, peach and pear trees. This will not only increase the yield but will also eliminate alternate-year bearing, which is the problem when a fruit tree bears heavily one year and has little or no fruit the next.

Some home fruit growers inadvertently thin their trees every spring by using Sevin, which kills the bees needed for pollination. Do not apply Sevin from the time the trees bloom to five weeks after bloom.

Peaches should be thinned four to six weeks after bloom. There should be four to six inches between each fruit. Apples and pears should be thinned between 30 and 60 days after bloom. There should be six to eight inches between each fruit.

Late May, around Memorial Day weekend, is the time to spray Lindane on your beloved dogwood trees to kill the dreaded dogwood borer, an insect that often damages our favorite spring tree by eating holes into it.

Check your tree regularly for the damage — holes and sawdust. Dogwoods grown out in full sun — they prefer to be understory trees — seem more vulnerable to the borer. It can be controlled with sprays of Lindane along the trunk and lower limbs, which insures that the insecticide will be on the bark when the young borers hatch and begin entering the tree. Also, be sure to avoid attacking the shins of the dogwood with your lawn mower. Those gashes provide openings for disease. You can also spray for dogwood borers in August as a follow-strike, but May is best.

Check your roses to see if they are "going wild" — blooming from beneath the bud union or from their roots. That's not the growth you want on a hybrid plant.

This wild growth can occur when a bud union freezes or dies, or if the plant roots dry out. Wild growth will have smaller, light-colored leaves and should be cut away. Chances are the wild growth will produce an inferior plant; if you had a guarantee with your purchase, you should exercise it.

Late May is also the time when bagworm larvae begin to hatch and crawl out of their tiny bags in search of food. The larvae, the most common pests to evergreens in this area, can strip shrubs of all their foliage, even killing them. They will also attack maple trees, roses and flowering quince.

The bags are very small — you may have to search carefully to find them. If there are only a few on the tree, they can be removed by hand. If the infestation is heavy, they should be sprayed with Malathion, Orthene, diazinon or

Dylox, or the biological control, Dipel or Thuricide.

FRED'S TIPS

If you have a serious love for cucumbers and little room to grow them, you can nearly double your harvest by growing them in a wire cage or up a trellis.

A study at Louisiana State University indicated that fruit set almost doubled when the plants were allowed to grow up instead of out. The plants grew bigger leaves and had better access to the sun, and the amount of fruit rot was reduced.

You must help the plant tendrils get started on the wire. One week after they've begun to bloom, side-dress them with 1/2 cup of 10-10-10 fertilizer. Repeat in three weeks. Don't worry. The vines will be strong enough to support even big cucumbers.

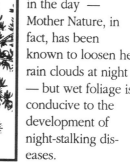

What type of flowers will do best in a hot, dry area or adapt especially well to a long drought? Around here, your best flowering bets are zinnias, ornamental peppers, cosmos, vinca, portulaca or moss rose, verbena, celosia or cockscomb, ageratum, cleome, gazania and gerbera. For the vegetable garden try okra, lima beans, amaranth, small cherry tomatoes and hot peppers. I had especially good luck with an ornamental pepper called "candlelight," an edible hot pepper.

Newspapers topped with grass clippings make an especially nice mulch because there is nothing to pick up after the gardening season is over; just let it decompose and plow it under. Even with the terrible summer of 1988 I only had to water my cherry tomatoes four times because we'd mulched so well. Don't use paper with color ink, however.

Black plastic will work in some areas but should not be used around permanent plantings like foundation evergreens. It will not decompose. It can suffocate root systems and makes the plants difficult to water.

When you do water, water deeply. Merely sprinkling the garden encourages shallow root growth, which is detrimental to your plants. Try to water early in the day. Sometimes you can't avoid watering late in the day — Mother Nature, in fact, has been known to loosen her rain clouds at night — but wet foliage is conducive to the development of night-stalking diseases.

In long periods of drought, soak your trees and shrubs thoroughly with a hose.

If your lawn is heavily shaded by large trees, especially maples, you will probably never get a strong stand of grass. My advice is to plant ground covers.

One of most attractive ground covers in our area is ajuga, or carpet bugleweed. Its glossy green foliage turns a bronzy green in the fall, and the plant has a show of bright blue flower spikes in late summer.

If you have a steep slope, liriope, also called lilyturf and monkey grass, has spiky blades eight to 12 inches tall. In July and August it sends up tall spikes of lavender or white flowers. It's tough, easily adaptable, winter hardy and divides easily if you want to start it somewhere else. There are whole sections of seed catalogs dedicated to ground covers, so check them out.

Cinder blocks will not only provide a retaining wall for your herb beds, but you can also plant herbs in the holes in the blocks, giving you a little more space to grow. Since most commonly grown herbs need a slightly alkaline soil — pH 7 to 8 — the blocks will constantly leach lime into the soil, helping to maintain the pH level. However, you will need a blend of topsoil, sand, sphagnum moss and a little agricultural lime as a soil mix for the blocks. You'll also have to water often because small patches of soil tend to dry out more quickly.

If you buy a flower or vegetable transplant in a peat pot, never, never let any part of the pot stick above the soil level when you put it in the ground. If you do, the peat pot will act as a wick, drawing moisture from the plant's soil and allowing it to evaporate into the air.

If you can't remove the peat pot because the plant's root system has grown into it, tear away the top lip of the pot so it will not be in contact with the air. I once saw a whole garden of peppers and tomatoes die because peat pots were not buried deep enough.

Every year I get calls from people who applied the wrong kind of chemicals to their garden and then wonder if they can still harvest their vegetables. The answer is always NO! They must start over again.

I cannot stress enough that you must read the labels on all chemicals and apply accordingly. If the label says a plant should not be picked for a certain time after spraying, don't pick it. If the label says one tablespoon is good, don't ever think two tablespoons is better. It's not. If you only follow one piece of advice follow that. Your health is at stake.

Many people will see an infestation of winged ants near their houses — especially during a warm spring — and fear the worst: termites.

The best way to tell the winged ant from the termite is to examine the wings. Termites have two pairs of wings of equal length. Flying ants also have two pairs of wings, but they are unequal in length. Also, the termite has a thick waist; the waist of a flying ant is pinched in.

If it still looks likes termites, don't panic. Termites work slowly. Call two or three pest-control companies for examinations and estimates. Be sure the firm is licensed and that its employees have ID cards issued by the state division of pesticides. Also, be sure to ask for references.

Old-fashioned manure is a good fertilizer that supplies mostly nitrogen to the soil. But spring is not the best time to apply manure because it often gives off ammonia that can "burn" plants and can even irritate the human who applies it. A good friend once had the hair on his arms singed by fresh ammonia. The best time to apply manure to the garden is the fall so it has time to cool down before going to work on plants, and letting it age under plastic will help, and improve the view.

If you bought ladybugs to release in your garden to control the bad bugs, you could be disappointed. The ladybugs may have "itchy wings."

According to the U. S. Department of Agriculture, mail-order ladybugs are collected from their hibernating quarters in California canyons.

These ladybugs don't come with a sense of duty or a road map. They will usually disappear, leaving your garden miles behind while searching for cultivated fields. The ladybugs you find in your garden are the local variety. The people your mail-order ladybugs visit after you release them will be grateful, but they won't know whom to thank.

Crab-apple trees in our area are susceptible to apple-scab disease if extended wet periods occur as the trees are developing leaves. Severely infected trees will show yellow leaves and suffer premature leaf drop. They can be sprayed with fungicides following wet periods, but the best and cheapest answer is to purchase only trees that are disease-resistant. Crab apples are lovely ornamentals, but only if you buy the right kind.

One handy way to remove the old blossoms from your azalea plant is with a broom. But be gentle, or you will damage the plant. It's also a good time to apply a high-acid fertilizer around the plants. Repeat in June. Keep them watered. Azaleas have shallow roots.

FRED'S SUPER TIP

It doesn't matter how good a gardener you think you are, the one vegetable we measure most gardeners by is the tomato.

The traditional time to plant tomatoes is after Derby Day. You can plant earlier, but chances are you'll be out there covering the plants on many frosty evenings.

If you buy tomato plants, choose short, stocky, healthy-looking ones, and buy a package of water-soluble tomato food like 5-10-5 while you're at it. A lot of people make the mistake of buying the biggest plant in the gardening center, the one that looks as if it might blossom first. It might, but in the long run a smaller, nicely shaped plant will bear more fruit.

Whether buying your seedlings or beginning them at home, choose varieties that say V.F.N. or V.F.N.T. That's not some sort of secret code. It indicates the variety's resistance to verticillium wilt, fusarium wilt, tobacco mosaic and nematodes (those small insects that attack root systems).

Also, consider the variety. A determinate tomato is one that will be bushy and not grow more than five feet tall. An indeterminate plant will grow taller and bloom all summer, producing new fruits until frost.

Check the number of days from first blooming to picking. Early Girl plants, for instance, will produce tomatoes in 54 days. Better Boy, one of the most popular varieties around here, will take about 70 days. Because there are dozens of varieties, you can have tomatoes from late June until frost if you plan carefully.

Another mistake home gardeners often make with tomatoes is not planting them deep enough. Any part of the stem without leaves should be planted under ground. One year I found a tomato plant with 12 inches of bare stem, and I buried it horizontally, bending the top upward so only its tip was above ground. New roots developed all along the stem, and it did very well.

For years now I've been growing my tomatoes in cages, and they love it. It eliminates the chore of tying the plants to the stake. They show less crack and sunburn, ripen more uniformly and produce fewer culls.

You can use concrete reinforcing wire for cages, but it will need painting. Old "hog wire" will make nice cages. The wire should be about 76 inches long, which will curl into a nice-sized cage, and 60 inches high. Anchor it with a stake.

The most important part of the whole tomato-growing season is using mulch. It's the best way to prevent blossom-end rot, that dark, leathery scar you will often see on the bottom of the tomato in hot weather. It's a disease blamed on a calcium deficiency in the soil because of constant fluctuations in soil moisture. Mulching helps prevent that.

Finally, you can't do much bragging about your tomatoes unless you can take one over to the neighbor's house. I had a call a few years ago from someone who followed my suggestion of caging tomatoes, only he had the hardest time getting them out of the cage. He'd used chicken wire.

June

✏️ June Checklist

LAWN TIPS

❑ Check your lawn for both narrowleaf and broadleaf weeds.
❑ Select either chemical or organic weed-control methods.
❑ More mowing — more watering.

EARLY

❑ Spray dogwoods to prevent borer infestation.
❑ Divide and reset irises.
❑ Set out caladiums, cannas and elephant ears.
❑ Renovate strawberry patch.
❑ Mulch garden.
❑ Plant Halloween pumpkins.
❑ Spray tomatoes with fruit-setting hormone.
❑ Prune privet hedge.
❑ Continue thinning fruit on trees.
❑ Inspect trees and evergreens for bagworms.
❑ Trim tops off peony bushes.
❑ Water garden and newly planted trees.

MIDDLE

❑ Prune climbing roses and apply fungicide.
❑ Stop harvesting asparagus and rhubarb.
❑ Start seeds (cabbage, broccoli and brussels sprouts) for fall garden.
❑ Rip out any spinach, radishes and lettuce that has "bolted" and plant beans or corn in its place.
❑ Pinch back mums, coleus and impatiens.

❑ Check cucumbers, melons and squash for cucumber beetles.
❑ Check tomatoes for early blight.
❑ Check a few potato plants for blackleg.
❑ Pinch faded blooms and seed pods off petunias, water and fertilize.

LATE

❑ Spray grass for sod webworms.
❑ Check pepper plants for bacterial leaf spot.
❑ Check houseplants and water often.
❑ Continue spraying fruit trees.
❑ Pick raspberries before they become overripe to avoid sap beetles.
❑ Check to be sure that potatoes, carrots and onions are covered with dirt.
❑ Remove foliage and transplant bulbs from spring-flowering plants.
❑ Remove suckers from tomato plants.
❑ Sow quick-growing annuals.

SUPER TIP

❑ Raising super roses.

June is the month when you can't see the trees for all the canning jars, kettles and preservatives stacked up on the kitchen table. All that time in the garden is paying off — with more time in the kitchen.

It's a month that was named for Juno, the Roman's patron goddess of marriage, although a second theory says June is taken from the Latin word juniores, or "young men," who were especially honored by the Romans in that month. Actually, both men and women get together for weddings in June — many of them outdoors.

The average high temperature in the Louisville area in June is 84 degrees; the average low 63.3 degrees. The average rainfall is 3.60 inches, a drop from March, April and May.

The wettest June in Louisville history was the 10.11 inches that fell in 1960; the driest was the .35 inches in 1936. In Kentucky lore, however, that palls to the 10.40 that fell on little Dunmor in one 24-hour period on June 28, 1960.

Scottsville, Ky., won a spot of dubious distinction on June 23, 1969, when 8.85 inches of rain fell on the city in just six hours. That's a lot, but on June 26, 1943, Berea College in Eastern Kentucky recorded 3.87 inches of rain in one hour.

The warmest June day on record was June 28, 1944, when the thermometer hit 103. The coldest was June 1, 1966, when the temperature hit 42 degrees and 300,000 tomatoes left for Florida.

There are 14 hours and 38 minutes of sun on June 1, and 14 hours and 47 minutes on June 30. The longest day of the year is June 21 when the sun is up 14 hours and 49 minutes. The average soil temperature in June ranges from 75 to 83 degrees.

Kentucky became the 15th state to join the union on June 1, 1792. Jeff Davis, president of the Confederacy, was born in Kentucky on June 3, 1808.

LAWN TIPS

It's June, time for a heart-to-heart talk about the second enemy of a blue-ribbon lawn: weeds.

Weeds, like dumb ideas, are everywhere and just about as harmful. Short of baking every square inch of dirt in your yard in a 550-degree oven for 45 minutes to sterilize it, weed seeds are found in dirt from the soil's surface to a depth of 6 to 7 inches.

Some will wait there for years for just the right combination of heat, light and water to blast through to the top. Agronomists, in fact, estimate there's at least one weed with your name on it in every square inch of soil, and probably a lot more.

Even if your lawn was developed from the very best sod, weeds are a threat. They blow in on the wind from the neighbor's dandelion patch. Birds flying overhead drop weed seeds. A heavy rain will wash them in from an uphill slope. Some even come in from the seed you bought at the store if you grow your lawn from scratch.

Once in or on your lawn, weeds benefit from the relentless digging of worms and insects, or a heavy rain, to get lodged in the right place. Most become established in late winter and early spring, another reason to start a new lawn in the fall when competition is at a minimum.

There are two types of weeds: narrowleaf and broadleaf. Narrowleaf weeds are often other grasses, such as the dreaded quack grass and crab grass. Broadleaf weeds include all non-grassy weeds such as dandelions, chickweed, plantain and spurge.

I hate to keep playing the same garden record over and over, but the central truth of Good Lawn Care holds here too: A thick, healthy lawn, one that has been properly fertilized, mowed and watered, is the best answer to weed control.

The second best answer, my fellow Americans, is constant diligence.

Again, herbicides should only be used as a last resort. If used in excess, or at the wrong times, herbicides can also kill many of your valuable flowers and shrubs. Heavy residues may end up on the feet of any creatures — or people — that pass by. The objective of chemical weed control is to eliminate the most weeds with the minimal amount of use.

Pre-emergent control kills sprouting weeds as they reach the surface. Many pre-emergents are granular and must be watered into the soil. Always apply herbicides on calm days. Never reuse the containers used for mixing herbicides, or the cans or bottles in which you bought the herbicides.

Every herbicide container has a label with very specific directions, a list of weeds on which it is effective, the active chemical ingredients and a description of how harmful it might be to turf grasses. Be sure you know how long the herbicide ingredients remain active before using it. Some herbicides are restricted in some areas and cannot be used without a permit, which is only issued after you have taken a lesson from an agricultural organization on how to properly use the herbicide.

Weed identification is very important. Some weeds — such as dandelions — are easy to spot. Others take a little work. If you're not certain what you've got, pick off a few weeds and take them with you to your county extension office or a reputable nursery, where they often have large color pictures of the enemy.

Herbicides work best when the weeds are actively growing, so a drought, or tough conditions, will make weeds all the tougher to eradicate. Herbicides are designed to kill weeds without harming your grass. While they kill selectively, they can cause minor damage — like yellowing — to grass.

A non-selective herbicide — Roundup, for example — will kill everything: weeds, grass and any flowers that were accidentally sprayed. Such herbicides are useful if you want to totally renovate your lawn or if you want to kill an area of your lawn that has been taken over by weeds. But they must be used with great care.

I always use a separate sprayer — and mark the word POISON on it very carefully — when using any total-kill herbicide. It's also very important to rinse the sprayer very carefully after every use.

Here's a list of weeds you should look for in your lawn and some herbicides to deal with them — as a last resort:

CHICKWEED — Some springs it seems chickweed will grow so thickly it covers everything in sight. It's an annual that forms a tight mat of succulent, reddish-purple stems with small, smooth leaves. It's a cool-weather weed, often slowing down in summer's heat, but what a mess it can cause in your perennial beds and lawn edges until then. Because it becomes so intertwined with plants you care about, it's best weeded by hand — or with a snow shovel. There are herbicides that can be used with great care. Read the bottle labels for the right one.

CRAB GRASS — Just the very words crab grass conjure up images of an evil invader with long pincers and a terrific appetite for a manicured lawn. As mentioned in previous chapters, crabgrass seeds normally begin to germinate in early spring. The seedling is small, almost harmless-looking, but with summer's fierce heat it soon develops into a plant that can easily crowd out tall fescues and bluegrass.

Since the seed needs a lot of water, frequent rainfall or too much light irrigation is part of a recipe for disaster. Lawn fertilization in late spring or early summer often helps the crab grass more than the lawn grass.

Once it's established it may be there for life because it will seed the surface, then ready itself for next year's germination. It's best handled with a pre-emergent herbicide in the early spring, about the time the forsythia are in bloom. Although it's not always as successful, there are also herbicides that will kill crab grass after it has emerged, but they may also yellow other grasses. Any reputable nursery will stock them.

DANDELIONS — Although possessing a certain elemental beauty, especially as their airy seeds take flight, dandelions are perhaps the most visible — and thus annoying — weed. They are perennials, and once they are established they develop roots that seem to bore at least 15 feet into the ground.

In smaller areas, it's often easiest just to dig them up, taking great care to haul out the roots with the tops. Failing that, an application of a 2,4-D weed-killer in spring or fall will eliminate them from your yard.

But if the neighbor allows his dandelion seeds to take flight, you may as well prepare for a lifetime battle.

PLANTAIN — Plantain is another perennial that grows from seed. It has flat, wide, green leaves, often sending up a tall, spiky seed head that distinguishes the plant. Plantain often appears in big colonies, sometimes so thick it chokes out grasses below its broad leaves.

If you cut off the spiky head, another will grow in its place. It, like dandelions, can be handled with a broadleaf herbicide such as 2,4-D.

QUACK GRASS — Another perennial, quack grass has rhizomes that spread quickly when nearby soil is cultivated. Even worse, if the rhizomes are cut into small pieces, additional plants will grow from them. The best quack-grass control is to weed it out as you see it. If the infestation becomes too serious, you may need a total kill such as Roundup. It will get rid of everything — grass and weeds — and you'll have to begin over with a new lawn.

VIOLETS — Although often kind of pretty, wild violets in the lawn often give homeowners a headache. There are products such as Turflon II that can kill them, but they should be applied by professionals only. 3-4 applications 3-4 weeks apart will eliminate most violets.

WILD ONION — Another perennial that grows from seed into a thick clump of bulbs, wild onion is a pest in the spring when it sends up tightly knit bunches of green shoots that smell highly of — well — onion, when mowed. They are very good at crowding out lawn grasses and giving your lawn a raggedy, uneven look. It can be controlled with 2, 4-D herbicides labeled for wild garlic or onion.

MOSSES — One special problem of homeowners who have a lot of dense shade is moss, which forms a thick, almost indestructible mat in shady areas with poor drainage. Mosses can't really compete with grass; the grass just won't grow in those areas. Moss can be controlled with copper or ferasulphate, but it will come right back; it's the neighborhood that causes the problem and prevents control.

The only real answer is to cut away some of the limbs that are providing the shade, improve soil drainage, improve the soil or just learn to live with it. Moss does have a certain beauty.

GARDEN TIPS
EARLY

Unless you did it around Memorial Day, you'd better hurry to protect your precious dogwood trees from the dogwood borer with sprays of Lindane.

The borer is a major problem for dogwoods, and it is a particular pest if the dogwoods are in full sun. A University of Kentucky study showed that the probability of dogwood-borer in festation was 68 percent in full sun, 50 percent in partial shade and 21 percent in full shade.

Wounding, generally caused by lawn mowers, also increased the likelihood of infestation; up to 78 percent for severe wounding and 40 percent for slight wounding.

So it's best to plant dogwoods in the shade, mulch around the tree to avoid lawn-mower damage and use Lindane on the Memorial Day weekend, or soon afterward. Be sure to heavily wet the trunk from the soil line up to the bottom limbs.

A reminder that overcrowded clumps of bearded iris can be divided and reset during June.

Dig the clumps and wash them off with a hose to reveal rot or borer damage. Cut away any infected parts with a sharp knife and divide the healthy portions into single or paired rhizomes.

To prevent infection, dust the rhizomes with Captan before replanting. Cut the foliage in half, or shorter, and reset the rhizomes no more than one inch deep. Be sure the very top of the rhizome is at ground level. If it's too deep, the flower will not bloom properly.

Be sure to break the seed pods off the plants you don't move so their energy can be devoted to new growth.

The soil temperature should be warm enough to get those caladiums, cannas and elephant-ear plants into the ground. Don't plant them too soon; they don't like anything below 70 degrees and will refuse to grow if it's cooler. They need lots of water once they're in the ground.

Now that strawberry picking is over, it's time to wash the red stains off your fingers and renovate the patch for next year. With new plantings, the crop usually drops off after the second season, but you can help keep it vital by mowing the leaves to a height of two to three inches. As hard as it might be to do, you should also cultivate the space between the rows and thin the plants to about 18 inches apart. Then apply a general-purpose fertilizer between the rows at a rate of five pounds per 100 feet. Finally, the runners should be encouraged to root and form new plants.

A reminder that if you want to have ready access to your garden later this summer while your neighbor is wading around knee high in weeds trying to find his zucchini, it's time to put down mulch.

For as long as I've been doing the "Weekend Gardener," I've advocated using newspapers and grass clippings. Wet the papers first to make them easier to handle, then place them eight to 10 pages thick. Work soil around the edges of the paper with a hoe, then spread the grass clippings two to three inches thick. Don't use too much grass because it gets very hot as it decomposes. Keep adding clippings as the grass rots. At the end of the season, plow it all under.

As odd as it sounds, June is the perfect time to plant the perfect Halloween pumpkin. That's because many of the best pumpkins take about 90 days to mature. If they're planted in May, they will mature in August and may go soft by the time Halloween rolls around.

So check the growing days on the back of the seed package and plant accordingly. If pumpkins must be picked before Halloween because of a heavy frost, store them in a cool, dry place.

This is the time of year when home gardeners notice that the first blossoms are falling off their tomato plants, a crisis nearly as bad as the children growing up and leaving home.

This often happens when there are night temperatures below 60 degrees or on extremely hot days, neither of which are conducive to setting fruit.

Spraying the clusters with a fruit-setting hormone such as Blossom Set helps alleviate the problem and could give you tomatoes three weeks sooner than your neighbor, which is well worth the price.

Early spring is always the best time to plant or prune your privet hedges. If your 10-year-old privet hedge is looking scraggly and hopeless, it can be cut within six inches of the ground and retrained into a decent hedge. Privets can be cut just about anytime the shears are sharp. Be sure to prune it in "triangular fashion," thicker at the bottom than at the top.

If you notice your fruit trees are shedding small fruits this time of year, don't worry about it; the drop is just nature's way of taking care of overpopulation.

Most trees have at least two waves of fruit drop, the first right after blooming and the second three to four weeks later, often in June. Since only one bloom in 20 is needed for a good crop, the natural drop won't do much harm.

In fact, chances are you'll have to help nature along in June by thinning the apple crop to about one fruit every six to eight inches. Peaches and plums should be thinned to one fruit every four to five inches.

Early June is also the time to inspect your juniper, arborvitae and other trees for bagworms. They'll soon be hanging from the limbs in spindly shaped bags about two inches long. The bags contain worms that feed on a wide variety of deciduous trees and evergreens.

Pick off the bags you can reach and burn them or throw them in the garbage. If it appears that the worms have already hatched, spray with Sevin, Malathion or bacillus thuringensis, which is also called Dipel or Thuricide.

Be sure to snip those ugly tops off your peony bushes to get them on the road to beauty for next year. If your peony has been in the ground several years and still hasn't bloomed, chances are you planted it too deep. Mark it with a stick and make a note to replant it in the fall. A happy, blooming peony bush can go decades without being transplanted.

This is a critical time for watering the garden. Those long June dry spells can weaken plants so badly they might not recover. Your garden needs at least an inch or two of water every week. Occasional light sprinkling of the garden or the lawn does more harm than good.

Put a rain gauge next to your garden and if it's coming up short, break out the sprinkler.

Also, don't neglect newly planted trees, even the ones you planted last year. Death by drought can occur even two or three years later. Let the hose run over them for 20 minutes.

One of the more frustrating things for gardeners is having shrubs or perennials that don't bloom. Here are some old favorites and some possible reasons why they aren't blooming.

AZALEA AND RHODODENDRON — They need acid soil. Often a late spring frost will kill the buds. They need sun, preferably a morning sun, then filtered light the rest of the day. If the soil is too soggy, the roots may rot.

DAFFODILS — They can get too thick; they need to be divided every few years. You must allow the foliage to yellow and rot a little before mowing it down in the spring. That's when the plants build strength for the next spring.

FORSYTHIA — Pruning in midsummer or fall eliminated the blooms, which are set in the late spring to summer.

FLOWERING CRAB — A late spring frost will kill the buds. They can also be done in by poor soil drainage. Spray in the spring for fungal diseases that can damage next year's buds.

LILACS — A late spring frost, wet roots or soil that is too acidic can spell problems.

OAK-LEAF HYDRANGEAS — They need some sun, but too much will scorch the leaves. They need an acid soil. A late-spring frost will nip the buds.

PEONIES — If they are planted too deep or in an area that's too shady with too much competition from tree roots, you can have problems. Botrytis blight can kill the buds as they emerge from the ground.

VIBURNUM — It can be done in by soil that's too dry or not acid enough. It might also need more sun.

MIDDLE

Be sure to prune your climbing roses right after the blossoms fade and apply a fungicide to prevent and control black spot. If you cut some of your other flowers to take indoors, be sure you cut them again just before placing them in water and add a floral preservative to keep them fresh. Changing water frequently helps too.

You should have stopped harvesting rhubarb and asparagus by now to allow the plants to develop and store food for next year's asparagus salad or rhubarb pie. Fertilize and water to keep them going.

If you're thinking about a fall garden of cabbage, broccoli and brussels sprouts, now is the time to start your seeds. Use the same methods you used in the spring, only keeping the soil warm shouldn't be as much of a problem. Remember, it's only about 190 shopping days until Christmas.

Once we hit mid-June, all that lovely spinach and lettuce and those rows of radishes are going to "bolt" in the hot weather, turn ugly and go to seed. You might as well rip them out, refertilize and consider second plantings of beans or corn in the same place.

One sure way to get bushier growth from your mums, coleus and impatiens is to pinch back the shoot tips. It's especially important to pinch back the mums now, or they will be too leggy this fall.

Mid-June is the time you may notice that some of your cucumber, melon and squash plants are dying for no apparent reason. The culprit is often the cucumber beetle, a black-and-yellow striped vermin that carries a disease called bacterial wilt. There IS no known cure, so spray your plants regularly with Sevin to control the pests.

If the weather has been warm and very moist, check your tomatoes for early blight, a disease that first appears as circular to angular brown or black spots on the lower leaves. Pinch off the leaf and apply a fungicide like Maneb.

The same kind of weather will produce blackleg on potato plants, an awful disease in which the stems turn black from the ground level up into the plant. As it spreads, the plants turn yellow and die. There's no cure for blackleg. Check the plants at random and dig up the diseased ones, use certified seed potatoes next time and don't plant potatoes in that spot for at least a year.

The petunia is one of those flowers that looks so nice when you bring it home but a month later is about as appealing as a dead dust mop. The secret to petunias is regular care. Keep the faded blooms pinched off, but don't just pull off the flower. You must also pinch away that tiny seed pod at the base of the flower or that stem will die back as the seeds ripen.

Be sure to water often and fertilize lightly every third week with a high-phosphorous fertilizer like 5-10-5 or 5-10-10. Plants that become too leggy by midsummer can be cut way back, and they will bloom until fall.

LATE

Late June is one of the two times to spray your grass for the sod webworm, the insect that often causes brown, unsightly patches in your lawn. When mowing you may see an increase in the number of small, gray moths that get up in front of the mower and "skitter" over the top of the ground. That's the female moths dropping their sod webworm eggs onto the soil. It's also time to spray with diazinon, and be sure to water it into the soil. Mid-August is the second time to spray.

Hot, rainy June weather can also produce bacterial leaf spot in peppers. The disease looks like brown or tan spots on leaves, which then turn yellow and fall, often leaving a carpet of leaves below the plant. It can be controlled with sprays of fixed copper every seven to 10 days.

Be sure to keep a close eye on the houseplants that have been set outdoors. They should be growing vigorously, will need more water than they did in doors and don't want direct, scalding sun.

Be sure to continue your fruit spraying schedule. As the fruit develops, you may have to prop up some of the limbs to keep them from breaking off. It takes a lot of work to keep a good home orchard going.

If you notice tiny black bugs on your raspberries, they're probably sap beetles, which literally make a living from overripe fruit The obvious solution is to get those berries off the bush and into your mouth, or freezer, as quickly as possible.

Check your potato plants, the sensitive shoulders of your carrots and even your onion bulbs to be sure they are covered with dirt. If you don't, the potato tubers will turn green and become inedible, and the carrots and onions will taste bad. Also, keep a constant check for potato beetles. Thiodan is the best bet to kill them.

By now it's safe to remove all the yellow foliage from the spring-flowering bulbs, if you haven't already done it. The bulbs can also be transplanted now, but be sure to add some bone meal or fertilizer. If you wait to transplant, you'll probably forget where they are.

Although not vital to the health of the plant, removing suckers from tomatoes will help preserve their energy and produce more fruit. Suckers, the big shoots that develop sideways from the main stem, can be picked off and rooted in sand or peat moss to get you going on a fall garden. I know one gardener who buys three tomato plants in the spring and winds up with a dozen or more just by rooting the suckers.

June is a great month to sow some quick-growing annuals like marigolds, ageratum or zinnias from seed. That way you'll have fresh flowers just about the time the other annuals are pooping out. Just be sure to mark the spot so they don't get lost in the jungle.

FRED'S TIPS

Here's a reminder that spraying with insecticides — especially Sevin — should be done in late afternoon or evening when the bees have gone home for the day. The bees are vital to the transfer of pollen that produces the fruit, and they are very susceptible to Sevin.

Horticulture advisers at the University of Kentucky have begun to notice that many newly planted trees and shrubs do not grow properly because their roots have been balled in synthetic burlap.

Natural burlap will decompose quickly, allowing the roots to spread. But the synthetic, plastic like material may last for years, inhibiting root growth. So check the wrapping around your dismal-looking plant, and if it feels and looks like plastic, you will have to dig up the plant, remove the synthetic material and replant the tree. Be sure to wait until fall, however, before doing this.

You'll see a lot of nurseries and discount stores offering sales on trees this time of year, but this late in the season is a very risky time to plant, and most places will not give guarantees with their sales. You're better off waiting until fall.

If you want to take a chance, buy some potted plants and shrubs at discount prices, nurse them through at home until planting time in the fall. Keep them very well-watered, and in partial sun. You might even heel them into a trench in the ground, still in the container.

You can save a lot of money buying bargains, but you may need it for funerals.

One strong word about the "topping" of large trees such as maples: DON'T.

That kind of topping, which many homeowners believe will save time picking up fallen limbs, severely weakens a tree, and the tree could be blown down in the next storm. Topping a tree only stimulates dozens of new shoots, none of which are as strong as the originals. Just don't do it.

One common belief among gardeners is that squash should not be planted next to cucumbers, muskmelons or watermelons because they will cross-pollinate, producing a strange-tasting fruit. That is not true. Any cross-pollination will affect the seeds produced by the fruit and not the taste. If you save those seeds, however, and planted them the following year, you might come up with a muskcumber.

This is the time of year when gardeners often complain that their squash is putting out lots of flowers but no fruit. The reason is that baby squash plants often produce mostly male flowers — with the female flowers to follow.

If you don't know the difference, look below the flower; the female flower will have a swollen ovary or a tiny squash. The male does not.

Here's something to keep you going while you're waiting. Pick some male blossoms. Mix one tablespoon of water with one egg and beat well. Add salt and pepper to flour or cornmeal. Place cooking oil in deep-fryer or use 1/4 cup of cooking oil in an iron skillet.

When the oil is hot, dip the blossoms into the egg mixture, roll them in the flour and fry them separately until brown. The taste is similar to mushrooms.

Don't overfertilize peppers and other "leafy" vegetables with nitrogen or you'll end up with beautiful foliage and no fruit. You must also harvest peppers regularly, or they will stop producing.

If you have a mouse-chasing cat around your house, here's a way that feline can help with gardening: Save your empty cat food cans and use them as a defense against cutworms, those small, noxious grubs that will chop off your plants at the ground line.

The greasy-brown to gray grubs work at night after spending the day curled up in the soil. But if you cut the tops and bottoms out of the cans and cut the sides of the cans and then put them around your broccoli or cabbage plants like collars, the plants will be safer. Be sure the cans are buried about an inch deep.

If some of those spring thunderstorms are knocking down your peony bushes — and doesn't it seem as if there's always a bad storm the week they hit full bloom — try putting little fences around them in the same manner you cage tomatoes, only not as high. It works wonders.

Speaking of thunderstorms, the U.S. Department of Agriculture advises that a freezer fully loaded with crops from your garden will stay cold for one or two days in the event of a power failure. Even if the meat and poultry have thawed, the USDA says you can refreeze them provided the meat and poultry still have ice crystals or have stayed below 40 degrees for less than two days. Just don't open the door every 45 seconds to check.

Ticks are a summer problem no one really likes to talk about, so let's get this over quickly. To remove a tick from the skin, grasp it as close to the skin as possible and pull upward, using steady, even pressure. Don't jerk it or twist it.

Now here's the really bad news: Keep the tick in a jar. Ticks can cause disease, and if the person bitten by the tick gets sick in a few weeks, the captured tick may help doctors identify the problem.

All right, we've talked about ticks, so let's do chiggers and get it over with. Chiggers, as every gardener knows, are what cause those red, itchy spots about an hour after you're back in the house. They are actually little insects about 1/15 of an inch long that live in tall grass. Their instincts are to rush to bite people where clothing fits the tightest, such as waistbands, or worse.

Chiggers don't burrow into the skin. They bite, feed, remain on the skin surface and fall off, only you don't know they were there until they are gone.

Use insect repellent before going out and take a hot, soapy shower when you come back in side. Several skin ointments can also reduce the itching.

A guaranteed way to increase your houseplant population comes from the Purdue University department of agriculture.

June, it says, is a great time to propagate indoor plants. As the days grow longer and brighter, houseplants put on a good flush of growth, and the actively growing tips make the best material for cutting.

The best plants to use are the easily rooted varieties such as coleus, wandering Jew, philodendron, ivy and peperomia, but don't hesitate to experiment with others.

Or if you want to be more adventurous, you can propagate the dieffenbachia (dumb cane) by cutting the stem into many sections, as long as each stem has one bud. And plants like jades and African violets can be propagated by rooting a single leaf.

To root these cuttings, place them in a clean container filled with moist, porous media such as vermiculite, perlite or potting soil. Cuttings will root in plain water, but the roots will be starved for oxygen and susceptible to root rot.

Enclose the cutting container in a perforated plastic bag to keep humidity high and prevent the plants from wilting. Keep the containers out of direct sunlight until the cuttings have rooted.

There is no need for fertilization during the rooting process, but be sure the media stay moist. Your new plants can be potted in a good quality soil mix as soon as the roots are an inch long.

FRED'S SUPER TIP

Roses are the queens of any summer garden, but many people are intimidated by them and let others enjoy all that royal elegance. Yes, roses do take a lot of work, but with regular care your garden can be as fragrant as any on the block.

So here are a few tips for summer rose care:

Roses need steady watering to bloom and remain healthy. Be sure they receive from one to two inches of water a week. If you are watering by hand, that's five to 10 gallons of water for a big bush and two to three gallons for a miniature.

Hot summer means "black spot," the persistent fungus that produces yellow foliage dotted with fuzzy black spots.

All nurseries have rose fungicides, and you'll never get through a season without them. Adding a few drops of dishwater liquid will help it stick to the bush.

Spider mites love hot dry weather and roses. If they're around, foliage on the lower part of the bush will appear dry and brownish-looking. The mites look like ground pepper.

You can wash mites away with a water wand early in the season, but if that's too difficult, use a commercial miticide.

Thrips, aphids, grasshoppers and Japanese beetles are the other insect pests that infect roses. They can and must be treated with regular use of Sevin and Malathion.

Apply special rose fertilizer every two to four weeks depending on its strength. Water the roses well before applying to prevent root damage. Be sure the fertilizer doesn't come in contact with the leaves, especially in hot weather, because it can burn the plant.

A layer of mulch from three to five inches thick is necessary to keep roses in form. Use pine bark, needles, oak leaves or newspapers.

Roses that are kept neatly pruned will consistently produce more flowers than bushes allowed to run wild. Cut the cane just a few inches below the faded bloom, and you will be rewarded with more flowers.

Many rose gardeners also remove most of the foliage at the lower end of the plant to improve air circulation and deprive spider mites of a place to roost.

Be consistent. This sounds like a lot of work because it is. But the fragrant rewards are well worth it.

July

◉ July Checklist

LAWN TIPS

❏ Control insects with proper mowing, watering and fertilizing.

❏ Chemical insect controls such as diazinon must be applied in late July or August.

EARLY

❏ Don't side-dress sweet potatoes.

❏ Fertilize hot peppers and okra.

❏ Spray magnolias for sassafras weevils.

❏ Check beans for bean leaf rollers.

❏ Pinch back, fertilize and mulch mums.

❏ Spray for Japanese beetles.

❏ Cut roses to take indoors.

❏ Cut day lilies for bouquets.

❏ Water ferns with a weak tea to replace acidity.

❏ Check for striped cucumber beetles and spotted cucumber beetles.

❏ Get rid of any squash infected with blossom-end rot.

❏ Check peach and nectarine trees for borers.

MIDDLE

❏ Thoroughly water trees and shrubs every week.

❏ Raise blade on lawn mower and change the oil.

❏ Clean out garden and plant fall crops.

❏ Remove seed pods and faded flowers from annuals.

❏ Check houseplants set outdoors.

❏ Water and fertilize indoor houseplants.

❏ Dig and divide iris.

❏ Check squash plants for squash-vine borer.

❏ Start biennials indoors to be transplanted to the garden in the fall.

❏ Mulch lima beans and check for Mexican bean beetles.

❏ Fertilize summer-flowering bulbs.

❏ Mulch, water and side-dress tomatoes.

❏ Check for azalea lace bug.

❏ Dig and divide day lilies.

❏ Check evergreens for bagworms.

LATE

❏ Check for parasitic dodder.

❏ Check lawn for whitish-gray slime.

❏ Check garden for sow bugs.

❏ Check for whiteflies.

❏ Check apple, pear and crab-apple trees for signs of fire blight.

❏ Water and fertilize fuchsias and check for whiteflies and spider mites.

SUPER TIP

❏ When to harvest your crops.

J uly is more of June, only worse. The heat is getting a little tougher to take, and the garden is just as demanding. Still, there are those quiet nights, when the sun dips down below the trees and you are alone with your sweet corn, green beans, early potatoes and late-evening thoughts, that it all seems worth while.

July was named for — and this shouldn't surprise you by now — Julius Caesar. July was first named Quintilis, which means fifth, because it once was the fifth month. But Julius Caesar made it seventh, and the Roman senate went along with it by naming the month Julius — which became July — in honor of him. Roman senates could do that kind of stuff.

The average high temperature, in Kentuckiana in July is 87.6 degrees; the average low 67.5. The average monthly precipitation is 4.10 inches, but in 1875, a record year, 16.46 inches of rain fell in Louisville. The lowest July rainfall was .25 inches, which fell, sorta, in 1930.

July thunderstorms left their mark in Lexington, where on July 3, 1931, 1.54 inches of rain fell in 15 minutes, and in Louisville, where 2.66 inches fell in 30 minutes on July 18, 1971.

As absolutely miserable as the summer of 1988 was overall, its July readings of 103 degrees still didn't set a record for the month. That pleasure went to July 24, 1901, July 28, 1930, and July 14, 1936, when the temperature hit 107 degrees in Louisville. The lowest July temperature ever was 49

degrees on July 24, 1947.

The hottest day ever in Indiana was the 116 degrees registered in Collegeville on July 14, 1936.

And the hottest day ever in Kentucky? On July 28, 1930, the thermometer hit 114 degrees in Greensburg in Green County.

There are 14 hours and 47 minutes of sun on July 1, and 14 hours and 10 minutes on July 31 as the growing seasons begins to creep away toward the west. The average soil temperature is between 77 and 85 degrees.

P.T. Barnum, a man who knew his nuts and bananas, was born on July 5, 1810, and author Henry Thoreau, who moved to the edge of Walden Pond to write of man and nature, was born July 12, 1817.

LAWN TIPS

Having guided you through the trials and tribulations of lawn diseases and weeds, we will deal in July with perhaps the worst menace of all: insects.

You'll never get rid of all your lawn bugs. There's no need to even try. Some are very beneficial, attacking the bugs that will damage your lawn.

Outside of those dead patches in your lawn — nature's way of telling you that white grubs may be at work — it's often very difficult to spot insect problems in a lawn. Insects have very complicated life cycles, often spending only a part of their development lunching on your grass.

The harmful pests come in three groups.

There are "sucking" insects such as chinchbugs, leafhoppers and spider mites that suck the liquid from the leaves, often leaving large, dry, yellow patches. These insects can often be found at the outer edges of those patches where the grass is just beginning to yellow.

The second group is often the larvae of moths, which appear as wormlike grubs on the grass surface. These include two particular pests: cutworms and sod webworms. The adult moths don't feed on the lawn, although they can often be seen flitting about the lawn surface, perhaps with some hungry birds in hot pursuit.

The last category is the one we are probably the most familiar with: underground pests such as white grubs. You may not be able to see these grubs, but other living things can help you spot insect infestations. If you see an abnormal number of birds feeding on your lawn, or see a great amount of skunk or mole damage, those are good indicators the noxious insects are seriously undermining your lawn.

Because the symptoms can look the same — large hunks of brown to yellow grass — it's not always easy to tell if your lawn is being damaged by disease or by grubs. But if patches of yellow or dying grass pull up easily like rolling up a rug, chances are you will find white grubs lurking under its surface.

Weeds are very seldom damaged by either diseases or insects, but they will quickly invade any grass area that's been damaged. Nor will chemical control of insects repair the damage done to your lawn. You're going to have to renovate the area, then reseed. And very late summer to early fall is the very best time for that, as you will see in subsequent chapters.

But in most cases, insect damage will be minimal; the grass will simply repair itself, filling in the spots with new growth.

The best way to control insects is to water, mow and fertilize properly. Ironically enough, a super-rich, overfertilized lawn is often the first place insects such as grubs will attack. The insecticide diazinon is effective against virtually all lawn insects, but it must be used with care and applied at the times of year when it will do the most good. Late July and August, for example, are the best times to use diazinon on white grubs.

Other chemicals are also effective on other insects, but only with modifiers. Some must be watered into the turf; others should only be applied when the turf is wet. Most of the chemicals are fast-acting and have a short residual effect. When in doubt, consult a qualified landscape horticulturist.

Here's a quick look at the worst of local lawn insects, all of which can be treated with diazinon.

CHINCHBUGS — The chinchbug is a small, sucking insect that feeds very nicely, thank you, on Kentucky bluegrass, fine fescues and Southern bentgrasses. In early life chinchbugs are red with a white band around their bellies; later they turn an orange-brown to black with white wings.

The bugs have a salivary fluid they inject into the grass stems, causing wilt or death. Damage is heaviest in sunny locations during hot, dry periods. That means that homeowners often have a difficult time distinguishing the chinchbug damage from drought-related damage.

CUTWORMS — A grayish, worm-like creature that is the larvae stage of a flying, beetle-like creature that leaves yellow spots on the grasses and plants it eats. One way to check for cutworms, along with other insects, is to cut the top and bottom from a coffee can and shove it deep into the ground, leaving just a little above the surface. Then flood this cylinder with water. Noxious creatures such as chinchbugs and cutworms will float to the surface.

SOD WEBWORMS — Sod webworms also like Kentucky bluegrass and fine fescues. They are the larvae stage of a buff-colored moth that hides during the day but flies at dusk dropping eggs at random over your lawn like adolescent bomber pilots.

The webworms develop dark brown heads and have spots all over their bodies. They construct silk-lined burrows through the thatch and upper soil, feeding at night on the grass leaves and stems near the surface. If as many as 15 larvae per square yard are spotted, insecticide is recommended. Water the grass before applying .

GRUBS — Grubs are the really bad guys of the turf world, feeding on Kentucky bluegrasses, fine fescues and tall fescues. There are many flying insects that produce these noxious critters, including the double-dreaded Japanese beetle, which spends about 10 months of the year in its underground phase as a grub. Other insects who develop the characteristic "C" shape of the grub include the June beetle, the "white grub" of the chafer beetle and the scarab beetle.

Since some beetles produce two generations of young a year, grubs are particularly damaging to grassroots. They feed most intensively in August, September and October.

When they are active, the lawn has a soft, spongy feel to it and can easily be pulled from the soil, revealing the culprits. Infested areas will develop patches of brown, then die. It is very important to treat these grubs with chemicals when they are active in late summer. Read the label on the insecticide bottle and follow the directions carefully.

GARDEN TIPS
EARLY

Now that early July has arrived, here's something you should NOT being doing: fertilizing or side-dressing your sweet potatoes.

Sweet potatoes love hot weather, but too much fertilizer, especially nitrogen, will produce long, thin fruit that look like sweet pencils. So remember to water, and you can trim back the vines a little if they grow too wild, but they don't need fertilizer.

Two vegetables that will profit from warm-weather fertilizing are hot peppers and okra. Give them 1/4 cup of 10-10-10 fertilizer per 10-foot row and repeat that every four to six weeks. Be sure to keep picking the fruit, too, because if you don't, the plants will pout and quit producing.

Every once in awhile in early summer I get calls from people who want to know what causes the holes in the leaves of their magnolias. The culprit is often the tiny sassafras weevil, which also goes by the alias magnolia leaf miner.

The weevils often feed in early July, then drop to the ground to spend the winter hiding there. You can lay them away permanently now by spraying with Sevin.

Check your beans now for one of the more curious bugs you will ever see — the bean leaf roller. The roller is actually a blue-green caterpillar with a big, black head and a bad attitude. It feeds on bean leaves, which it will neatly cut and fold over to form a tent that would make a Boy Scout happy. If there are not too many of them, they are fun to watch. If they become pests, Sevin will solve the problem.

Mums should be pinched back three or four times during the summer to make them more bushy when show time arrives in the fall. If your plants have be come too leggy, try rooting some of the longer clippings in pots and starter soil.

You can also promote better buds in the established plant by using a low-nitrogen fertilizer like 5-10-10. Use 1/2 cup per square yard and be sure to water in the fertilizer. Mulch will also keep mums healthy in the hot summer months.

Healthy roses can be enjoyed twice this time of year; once in the garden and later indoors. Be sure you cut the roses properly to ensure more flowers. Roses have either three, five or seven leaflets on each stem. Cut the stem so that at least one bunch of five or seven leaflets remains immediately below the cut. This will guarantee more flowers, not just more foliage.

Use a sharp knife, make the cut at an angle and submerge the cut roses in a pail of warm water. Once inside, remove all foliage that will be beneath the water line in the vase. Recut the ends so they will absorb water more readily. Place them in a cool spot, possibly even in the refrigerator, to give them a "rest" before they are set out.

Speaking of cut flowers, the selfless day lily will also make a nice indoor bouquet if handled properly. Cut off a stalk with several buds, place it in warm water and remove the spent flowers as new buds open.

If your fern looks a little peaked these days, try giving it a spot of tea. Yes, that's correct, a spot of tea. Ferns thrive in a peaty-type soil that's high in acid. When we water ferns as often as they like, we often wash a lot of acidity out of the soil, which can be replaced with a drink of tea.

Just drop a tea bag in two quarts of water and pour it on the fern. I do this once or twice a year, especially when the fern fronds begin to turn a light green.

Oh yes, when it comes to pouring tea on your ferns, remember: They drink it straight up. Skip the cream and sugar.

Stay on guard against the striped cucumber beetle and the spotted cucumber beetle. They carry the bacteria that produces bacterial wilt, the leading cause of sudden death among cucumbers, cantaloupes and melons. The beetles can be controlled with Sevin, methoxychlor, Rotenone or diazinon if used every seven to 10 days.

Gardeners often call in early July to ask why their squash are rotting at one end. The problem is a disease called "blossom-end rot," which is different from the fungus of the same name that attacks tomatoes. With squash, the rot comes in the form of a grayish mold that begins at the blossom and consumes the whole plant. It's caused by hot, humid weather and uneven watering. There is no cure. Pick off all infected squash and throw them away.

The backyard peach or nectarine tree is often susceptible to borers that will girdle the tree, killing it. The borers are active all summer but can be controlled with a spray or "painting" of Thiodan about July 1, as well as Aug. 1 and Sept. 1. Mark those dates on your calendar.

If you find the leaves of some vegetables — like eggplants or tomatoes — mysteriously disappearing, look around for the blister beetle. It's black and gray, about 1/2 inch long, and will chew leaves until it defoliates the whole plant. It can be controlled with Rotenone or methoxychlor. The good news is that the bug's babies feed on grasshopper eggs. The bad news is that it's called a blister beetle because its juices, as a defense mechanism, will cause blisters on your skin.

There's not often a lot of color to be

found in midsummer, at least where shrubs and trees are concerned. But if you want color, here's a short list of shrubs and trees that will help light up your yard for the Fourth of July.

Try the Korean stewartia, littleleaf linden, silver linden (Japanese beetles are very fond of lindens) and the golden-chain tree, the latter a little beauty when in bloom but a little scruffy the rest of the time.

Other favorites are the clethra, trumpet creeper, golden-rain tree, sourwood, kerria, buttonbush, rose-of-Sharon, hydrangea, buddleia (butterfly bush), Bottlebrush buckeye, spireas, abelia and smoke tree.

MIDDLE

We won't forget the drought of 1988 for a long, long time. It caused damage to flowers, trees and shrubs that may haunt us for several years because the heat could have severely weakened many plants, especially newly planted ones. In fact, plants that barely make it through a severe drought may die the following winter, especially if the winter is severe. Keep that in mind if some of your shrubs mysteriously refuse to come alive next spring.

That's why it's more important than ever to water weekly all summer unless Mother Nature does it for you. For smaller trees, let the hose run for 15 to 20 minutes to give them a good soaking. Don't just lay the hose against the trunk. The roots extend as least as far as the tree's drip line and possibly twice that far, so move the hose around.

During the hot summer months, be sure to raise the blade on your lawn mower about an inch. This will allow the plants to grow strong and form roots. If you haven't had the lawnmower blades sharpened since spring, they're way overdue.

There's also a good chance you have 600 pounds of caked grass under the mower deck, and the mower might even need an oil change, a chore many homeowners tackle about once every 36 months. Take care of your mower, and it will take care of you.

If you haven't started that fall garden yet, you've still got time. Remove all the old crops and clean out all debris and weeds. Water the garden thoroughly and allow it to dry so it's not muddy. Next, apply one pound of 10-10-10 or 12-12-12 fertilizer per 100 square feet of planting area. If the previous crop grew well, you may not need much more fertilizer. You can plant all the same warm-weather crops you planted in the spring. Refer to the chart we have in this book for suggested planting dates, but remember, those are just rough dates; no two years are the same.

One trick for increasing germination in warm weather is to dig a furrow and flood it with water two or three times. Then sow the seeds in the furrow and cover them with the soil you removed. Water will rise from the lower soil levels by capillary action and keep the seeds moist for several days. After a few days, resume normal watering.

Continue to pick faded flowers and seed pods from your annuals, especially marigolds, cosmos, snapdragons and zinnias. Cut all the long, scraggly stems off your petunias. Use a fungicide to control powdery mildew on zinnias and phlox. If your salvia are looking bleak and faded, trim off the old flowers with clippers. The plant will produce new ones by fall, and they'll be especially bright in the cooler weather.

Be sure to check daily on house-plants set outside for the summer. They can be severely damaged in just one long day of heat. It often helps in hot weather to dig a trench and bury the pots to protect the sensitive roots.

Houseplants are also susceptible to insect attacks and mildew. Those plants in clay pots might need watering twice a day. While you're at it, keep an eye on the houseplants you left indoors. They need regularly watering — and fertilizer too.

Irises that haven't been divided in five or six years can be dug, divided and replanted before Aug. 1. It sometimes helps to dip the plants in a bucket of water before dividing them to make them more pliable. It's also time to divide Oriental poppies and bleeding hearts, but only after the foliage dies back.

Check your squash plants for the squash-vine borer, a white, grublike caterpillar that bores into the fruit by tunneling through the vine. Unfortunately, the first sign of the borer is a sudden wilting of an apparently healthy runner. If the vine is infested, the best answer is to slit the stem and kill the borer with a wire. But it can be controlled with regular use of methoxy-chlor, Thiodan or Rotenone.

July is a good month to start biennials such as hollyhocks, foxglove, honesty, wallflowers and Canterbury bells from seed indoors. The seedlings will be big enough to transplant outdoors this fall, and you'll have great flowers next spring.

You may not like to sit out under a hot summer sun, but your lima beans love it. But they are extremely sensitive to root injury when in bloom, so apply-ing mulch in July is very beneficial. If you side-dress with fertilizer between the time the flowers bloom and the pods form, you'll not get the best fruit. Use Sevin to control the Mexican bean beetle.

Your summer flowering bulbs such as lilies should be in bloom now. They can be helped with a light dusting of 5-10-10 or 10-10-10 fertilizer but avoid a high nitrogen fertilizer because it can cause bulb decay. As the flowers fade, cut them off to prevent seed formation.

Remember, tomatoes, the vegetable gardeners most like to brag about, are susceptible to a bushelbasket full of problems in hot weather. Tomatoes will suffer blossom-end rot, cracked skin, sunscald and leaf roll. The trick to avoiding these ills is even watering, mulching and side-dressing with ammo-nium nitrate after the fruit has set. Scatter one tablespoon in a 6- to 10-inch circle around each plant. Repeat every two weeks.

It's time to keep a sharp eye out for the azalea lace bug, a pest that despite its aristocratic name can cut some real blue-collar holes in your azaleas and rhododendrons. So if the leaves of your plants are spotted and have brownish specks on the under side, it's time to spray them with Malathion or Sevin. With a severe infestation, it might take two or three applications seven days apart. And keep watering those azaleas and rhododendrons, especially the newly planted ones; they have very shallow root systems.

I've often called day lilies the lazy man's flower because they aren't fussy about sun, water or fertilizer and aren't bothered by insects or diseases. They are called day lilies because each individual flower only lasts one day. They should be dug and divided every four or five years, and the best time to do that is right after they are finished blooming — right about now.

Use a very sharp shovel and replant the clumps to the same depth. Dipping the plants in a bucket of water will also help in dividing day-lily clumps.

While you're at it, be on the lookout for the newer variety of day lilies that will bloom all summer. They're just coming onto the market.

Continue to look for the pesky bagworms, which will be hanging from your evergreens like Christmas tree ornaments. They especially like arborvitae and junipers. Pick them off, or use Sevin or Malathion.

LATE

The lovevine is at it again, making passes at all kinds of plants in the garden.

Lovevine is a common name for a parasitic annual called dodder. It looks like a very thin golden-colored string that winds itself around plants and chokes them to death. It's also called, less poetically, "strangleweed" and "goldthread."

There is no chemical way to discourage this lover of garden plants. The only way is to sit down and untangle it by hand. Take a stool to the garden with you. There are less pleasant ways to spend a summer evening. To insure the lovevine's demise, apply a pre-emergent weed control to the infected area late next spring.

In the warm, moist days of late July you may begin to notice slimy circles of mold from 1 to 24 inches in diameter forming on your lawn. Usually whitish-gray, but sometimes even yellow or red, slime mold looks ugly and permanent.

Fortunately, just like the Wicked Witch in the "Wizard of Oz," the slime can be easily washed away with a good splashing of water. Throw it from a bucket like Dorothy did, or just use the garden hose.

People often call or write asking about those gray, tank-like garden bugs that hide in shady, damp places and roll up like a ball when disturbed. They are sow bugs, also called "pillbugs," and are actually members of the crab and lobster family.

My grandfather used to call whiteflies "flying dandruff." They are the tiny, whitish insects which congregate under many leaves, especially those of tomato plants, and fly in great clouds from one plant to another when disturbed.

Orthene, Thiodan and insecticidal soap will control them. But since the flies are attracted to the color yellow, an organic way to get rid of them is to paint a board yellow, then coat it with a tacky substance, even motor oil. The whiteflies head for the yellow and get stuck. It's the 10-W-40 way to bug control.

Blackened twigs and branches on your apple, pear or crab-apple trees indicate they have fire blight. It will spread if not checked, so cut off the limbs below the infected area and destroy them. Be sure to disinfect the pruning tool between each cutting by dipping it in a solution of bleach and water; otherwise you will spread the disease. Spraying this time of year does not help.

Remember those fuchsias you bought this spring because they looked so cool, clean and pretty? Well, they will not survive the summer without daily watering and a high-phosphorous food

like 2-10-10 fertilizer. They also attract whiteflies and spider mites the way the ice-cream man attracts kids, so treat the insects with Orthene, Thiodan or insecticidal soap.

What the heck, treat the kids to ice cream too.

FRED'S TIPS

When harvesting corn, the ears should be snapped off the stalk with a downward push, twist and pull. Keep practicing the motion, and you might also develop a big-league curve ball.

Your pets are also bothered by insects — particularly fleas — during the hot summer months. They should be taken to the vet for regular checks and baths, but you should also be dusting them with powders and lotions available at pet stores.

The best way to water bigger trees and shrubs is with a special "soaker hose." They may cost a little more but are worth it because they allow the water to slowly seep into the ground. With a regular hose, the water may rush away from the tree roots and be wasted.

You'll get the most nutritional value from many vegetables — and often the best taste — by eating them raw. This includes peas, beans, summer squash, cauliflower, broccoli and even sweet corn. When you do cook them, try using as little water as possible. A vegetable "steamer" is the best.

While an insecticide will do some good even after the bugs have arrived, fungicides are different; they must be on the plant as a protective layer BEFORE disease strikes. They can't do anything to prevent disease once it has hit. Don't give up if you see evidence of disease; the fungicide can prevent future damage. But it can't cure what's already sick — or dead.

My wife and I raise quite a sizeable planting of blueberries each year, and I'm proud to say that we — not the birds — get all the crop. Our Save Our Blueberries (SOB) method involves metal rods used for electric fence, white PVC pipe and a roll of fruit-tree netting. I stake the metal rods along both sides of the patch, then use the hollow, bendable PVC pipe inserted on the rods to form arches. We secure netting to the PVC pipe with twist ties and leave enough netting at each end to use as flaps, which we secure with clothespins.

The type of arrangement you use will depend on the size of the crop you are protecting, but the same materials should work for a variety of berries that the birds like to share with man.

Rosie Lerner, a Purdue University extension horticulturist, says that a lemon-lime carbonated beverage makes a good homemade floral preservative. Lemon-lime pop provides citric acid to help prevent bacterial growth. It also provides sugar, which the flower loses as it ages. Do not use the beverage alone. Dilute it by half with water. Cut the flowers in early morning or late evening to get the maximum amount of water in the plant. Please, please, don't drink the water.

Those family photographs taken in the yard may be more valuable than you think. Landscape plants can add 25 percent to the market value of a house, and house damage caused by a falling tree may be covered by insurance. So while you're taking pictures, move around the yard, document every tree over six inches in height and store the pictures in a dark safety-deposit box next to the $1.5 million in cash. The pictures will help in making a claim.

Now that we're well into harvest season, why not keep a list — just for one week — of the amount of vegetables you take from your garden. Next time you go to the store, check the prices. It might be fun to see how much money your garden has saved you.

If your garden is plagued by continuous rainfall for several days, you can help the soil dry out by walking through the garden with a hoe or spading fork and opening the soil so the water can drain away. Just poking holes in the soil can help.

You'd think eggplant has feelings, and in a sense it does; it is very sensitive to cold water. To keep eggplant from sulking, keep it well-supplied with water that's had a chance to sit in the sun for a time. Often the water will warm up just being inside a hose out in the sun.

Cannas are tough enough to survive with little care and plenty of water. But they'll keep blooming longer if you remove the old flowering stalk just above the first set of leaves. Use sharp shears, and a new flower will bloom below the cut. To keep the plants lush, fertilize every few weeks with a 10-10-10 fertilizer. Dusting with Sevin will keep the leaf-roller caterpillar at bay.

Hostas, which like their shade, also respond very well to watering. A friend of mine has one growing in the shade near a downspout, and it's twice the size of any other. It produces better, and more fragrant, blossoms in early September, too.

If you divide your crowded Boston fern plants now, they'll fill out again by the end of the summer. Use a knife to divide the tough rootball into several sections. Plant each section in a suitable-sized pot and keep well-watered. Feed once a month during the summer. Use a water-soluble fertilizer like 18-18-18.

Some people occasionally try to rid their yards of poison ivy by burning it. Burning may work, but don't stand in the smoke. It can spread the poison just as readily as physical contact. Remember: To kill the weed, you must dig up the whole root system. Chemical control with Kleenup or Amitrol requires repeated applications.

If you think you touched the plant, wash the affected area with lukewarm water and a strong, alkaline laundry detergent. Then find some calamine lotion or hydrocortisone cream.

If you want to protect your indoor houseplants while you're on vacation, water them well, let the soil drain, and wrap the plants in a black plastic bag. That will prevent the soil from drying too quickly. Be sure to keep the bags out of direct sunlight.

If you're going to be gone for several weeks, trust your plants to a good, reliable neighbor. There aren't enough plastic bags in the world to replace one good neighbor.

FRED'S SUPER TIP

One thing many gardeners need to know is exactly when to harvest their crops, especially sweet corn and melons. Here's a brief list of the more popular crops:

Sweet corn should be picked when the kernels are milky. Pull back the shuck and squeeze a kernel with your fingernail. If the liquid is watery, the corn is not ready. If there's no liquid, it's ready for cattle feed. If it's milky, it's ready for the dinner table.

One other thing: The good gardener wears track shoes into the garden patch. Sweet corn should be in the kitchen to be cooked and served no longer than 9.8 seconds after it has been picked.

July and August are the months to harvest the onions you want to keep through the winter. The best time to harvest is when about half the tops have dried and fallen over. Waiting too long increases the chances of sunburn and decay. Use a spading fork to work the onions loose, let them dry in a dry, well-ventilated area for 10 to 12 days and store them in a cool, dry place.

Harvest cucumbers for slicing when they are at least three inches long, firm and have a good green color. If you plan to make pickles, harvest cucumbers when they are two to four inches long for sweet pickles, four to six inches long for dill pickles.

Green beans are most tender when the seed inside the pod is about one-third full size or begins to show through the pod. As the beans mature, the pods get more stringy.

Tomatoes should be evenly red but still firm to the touch. If you pick a day or two early, let them ripen at room temperature, but not in a sunny window. Do not store tomatoes in a refrigerator as it adversely affects the taste.

Begin to harvest beets when they are a little more than an inch in diameter and try to get the rest before they exceed three inches. Any bigger and they get pithy. Beet greens make good eating and can be harvested when the tops are big enough for cooking.

If you've been thinning carrots all along — and you should have been — you'll find that the longer they are in the ground, the tougher they become. In general — and carrots vary greatly in size and diameter — just pick them when they're the size you like to eat. Baby carrots are really yummy.

Dig potatoes when the tops yellow and die back. High soil temperatures can cause overripening. Avoid leaving spuds out in the sunlight. Baby potatoes can be dug by early July or several weeks after the plants have reached full growth. They are often the tastiest then. Be careful not to bruise the fruit.

Eggplant is edible from the time it is 1/3 grown until ripe and bright with color. Use it quickly because eggplant doesn't store well.

Pumpkins and winter squash should be harvested before the first frost, when the skin is hard and the colors darken. To avoid spoilage, do not pile them on top of each other.

Muskmelons should be harvested at the "full slip" stage, which loosely translates to the time when the plant will slip easily from the vine. However, the serious gardener must also solemnly "thump" the fruit to determine if it sounds ready.

Harvest green peppers when they are firm. If you want red peppers, just let them hang out there until the peppers turn red. Be sure to cut the peppers off the bush to save injury and to keep more peppers coming.

Sweet potatoes can be dug any time the tubers seem large enough. But they are very susceptible to frost, so a good trick is to cut away all the vines after the crop has fully matured. Since the vines often cover about 56 acres, it makes the digging much easier, too.

Watermelons can be taken into the kitchen when the underside turns from whitish to creamy yellow, the rind losses its gloss and appears dull, the stem dries up and the melon yields a dull "thud" when hit. If your hand goes into the melon to the third knuckle, you've got a problem. Another sure-fire method is to cut a "plug" from the melon and taste it when nobody is looking. Just be sure to put it back for another day.

August

✏️ August Checklist

LAWN TIPS

☐ Mow grass a little higher now to protect it from the heat.

☐ Check your lawn daily for grub and beetle damage.

☐ Mid-August to late September is the best time to start building a new lawn.

☐ This is also the best time to renovate existing lawns.

☐ Continue watering your lawn.

EARLY

☐ Water tomatoes and apply fungicides and insecticides.

☐ Check for powdery mildew.

☐ Cultivate cantaloupes with care.

☐ Fertilize amaryllis and snip off buds after blooms are gone.

☐ Remove old and rotting fruit from garden.

☐ Check beans for rust.

☐ Stop spraying fruit trees two weeks before harvest.

☐ Begin transforming luffa gourd into a sponge.

☐ Begin fall garden.

MIDDLE

☐ Cultivate night-blooming cereus.

☐ Do not fertilize trees and shrubs.

☐ Harvest grapes two to three weeks after color change.

☐ Decide what kind of bulbs to order to be planted in the fall.

☐ Prune and destroy all raspberry and blackberry canes that bore fruit.

☐ Take cuttings from annuals to start plants that will overwinter indoors.

☐ Pick dead buds off bedding plants to keep the plants blooming.

LATE

☐ Harvest pears when fruit changes color.

☐ Continue checking trees for bagworms and tent caterpillars.

☐ Plant "green-manure" crop to improve garden soil.

☐ If winter squash are ready, pick them and cure them in the sun.

☐ Don't prune landscape plants.

☐ Keep evergreens, trees and azaleas well-watered.

SUPER TIP

☐ A Japanese beetle primer.

August, with all its heat and droning crickets, brings us state fairs and a time to celebrate all that we have grown. It's the time when we become aware that the world has begun to reverse itself; the days are shorter, the nights are longer, and the occasional touch of autumn air is refreshing against the skin.

August was named for the great Roman leader Augustus, but the matter didn't stop there. That same Roman senate that named the month for Augustus stole a day from February and tacked it onto August to make the calendar work better. Don't you wish you could do that on Monday morning?

The average high temperature in Kentuckiana in August is 86.7 degrees, down slightly from July. The average low is 66.1 degrees. The average rainfall is 3.31 inches. Dry spells are common, but on one memorable August day, Aug. 29, 1917, .79 inches of rain fell on Louisville in just five minutes. That would have totaled 9.48 inches in one hour had it continued.

The record rainfall for the month was 10.53 inches, set in 1888. Seven years previous, in 1881, there was only .15 inches of rain, a record for the driest August.

The summer of '88 didn't break the all-time record for the single hottest day in August either. It reached 101 one day in August 1988, but it was 105 on Aug. 12, 1881, and on Aug. 5, 1918. The coldest August day ever was 45 degrees on Aug. 31, 1946.

There are 14 hours and eight minutes of sun on Aug. 1, and 13 hours and four minutes on Aug. 31. The average soil temperature ranges from 77 to 84 degrees.

William Clark, a leader of the Louis and Clark expedition and the brother of local hero George Rogers Clark, was born Aug. 1, 1770. The United States annexed Hawaii on Aug. 12, 1898, guaranteeing us good pineapples forever.

LAWN TIPS

It's show time! Up to now we've been mostly talking about taking care of an existing lawn. Mid-August to late September is the perfect time to do some serious work on building a new lawn — either totally from scratch or by repairing damaged areas in your old.

Much of this grass-growing information came from A. J. Powell at the University of Kentucky, who has put together two helpful pamphlets — AGF-50 and AGF-51 — that give plenty of user-friendly details about establishing a lawn and renovation. They and similiar pamphlets from Purdue University in Indiana are available at an extension service office near you.

So let's begin this month's discussion with what many people find to be the most daunting prospect of all: building a new lawn from scratch. It's really not that difficult. In fact, there is tremendous satisfaction in building a lawn from scratch, watching the bare ground being transformed before your eyes into thick, croquet-ready turf. So if you're at all tempted, give it a try.

We already told you that tall fescues such as Falcon and Rebel II — just to name II — are the best grasses for most Kentucky lawns even if Kentucky bluegrass seems a more obvious choice. In fact, another UK pamphlet, AGF-52, lists all the reasons you should pick a tall fescue; weather- and drought-tolerance being two of the best. Some of the other recommended tall fescue varieties were listed in the February chapter.

If you're totally fed up with the looks of your old lawn and want to start over, a chemical herbicide such as Roundup will kill off all the old grass. It will also — and this is very important — kill all vegetation it comes in contact with. So use it carefully or not at all.

You must allow about two weeks for the Roundup to kill all vegetation; an application made in early August should have you ready to plant new grass by mid-August. Why does it take awhile to work? You apply it to the foliage of the plant material you want to eliminate. The leaf tissue absorbs it, translocates it through the stem, underground and it begins to work by killing the plant's root system. So you do not get it in the soil at all which makes it environmentally friendly. Once the old grass is dead, you still must rake or till the area clean — thus baring the ground in preparation for the sowing of the new seed.

If chemicals frighten you, then tackle the old lawn the old-fashioned way; use a tiller to rip it all up. You can rent a tiller — or similar turf-tearing equipment — at a rental shop near you.

If your existing grass is very spotty, you can take a heavy rake and rip at the ground, pulling out all weak and diseased grasses. Either way you must not begin a new lawn until the seed is able to make full contact with the soil. Just tossing new grass seed onto an existing lawn won't get it. Nor, as the old wives' tale goes, will tossing grass seed onto snow so it can "melt" into the soil. Lawn rebuilding is a full-contact sport.

Alas, you may be building a new lawn in a bare-ground subdivision where the soil was mutilated, bulldozed and depleted during the construction process. Ask the contractor to pile all the topsoil over in a corner of the lot while the bulldozers are at work. Then it can be spread back over the homesite.

Failing that, large amounts of peatmoss, well-rotted sawdust or compost can help make your soil well again, but it takes a lot of time. The good news is that the tall fescue varieties of grass are very resilient; they will grow in the toughest of clays and the most porous of sand. The trick is to water well in summer drought.

In any event, you should always get your soil tested before seed planting so you know exactly what mixes of lime, nitrogen, phosphorous and potassium it needs to get well.

If that seems like too much trouble — or time is very short — a general guideline is to apply about 80 pounds of ground limestone per 1,000 square feet of yard, along with about 25 pounds of 10-10-10 fertilizer per 1,000 square feet. This should be worked into the top 4 to 6 inches of the soil before seeding. Grass is incredibly durable but you'll never have a blue-ribbon lawn without some blue-collar effort.

Seeding the prepared bed by hand is always fun — especially in a high wind, but the net result might be to improve a lawn two blocks away. More often that not, this "sidearm" grass-planting method produces wide streaks of thick grass, equally wide streaks of thin grass and large, embarrassing places with no grass.

Your lawn is a major investment in time, money and pride. If you want it to look good, buy a rotary seeder — you can use it later for fertilizing the grass — or rent one from the guy who rented you the tiller.

For the absolute best distribution you should seed your lawn from one direction — preferably upwind — then come back at a right angle to that. Follow the package directions; over-seeding may seem like the right thing to do, but it's counterproductive; the tiny plants will choke each other to death. Most lawn-seeding directions call for about six pounds of tall fescue per 1,000 square feet, so stick to that.

Once the ground is seeded, rake the soil lightly, then mulch — if feasible — with clean straw. This will protect the baby sprouts in their first few weeks in the bright, cruel world. About one bale of straw per 1,000 square feet is fine. Don't pack it tightly; leave room for the little guys to breath.

Water frequently and deeply. Let me repeat that with emphasis: WATER FRE-QUENTLY AND DEEPLY. Water is the one great key to getting a new lawn off and sprouting. Keep the area constantly moist — but not drowned — for 2 or 3 weeks.

Once the grass pushes up through the straw, mow the grass using a mower with a grass catcher attachment to pick up some of the straw along with the grass clippings. The rest of the straw will easily decompose. Don't rake up the straw or you could rake up the young grass plants too. As the new seedlings develop, mow them on a regular basis. Be sure the mower blade is about 2 1/2 to 3 inches high. A very light sprinkling of high-nitrogen fertilizer right after seeds pop up will help them fight weeds. You might want to apply another coating of a lawn starter fertilizer in late fall (November).

Weed control can usually begin, if needed, after the new seedlings have grown enough to be mowed twice. Before then the herbicides might injure their sensitive roots and blades. If you must seed during the spring — and fear crab-grass germination — you can apply a pre-emergent crab-grass killer at the time of seeding. Be sure the pre-emergent is labelled for use on a newly seeded lawn.

A quicker solution to all this is to buy sod and lay it down on your bare, well-prepared ground. It's more expen-sive, but when you add up time, labor and materials, the use of sod could actually be cheaper in many ways. Sod should be laid like bricks; the pieces should be "staggered" to give them greater strength. Use a sharpened concrete trowel to cut the pieces and to force the sod tightly together. Immediately after sod is laid it should be rolled with a roller, then saturated with water. Keep it moist until the underlying roots grow into the soil.

If your lawn is in bad shape, but you don't think totally rebuilding it is in order, you can just renovate it where it sits. The prime piece of rental equipment for that is a de-thatching machine, a near-medieval device whose knives or blades cut shallow grooves into the soil, ripping out dead grasses, weeds and thatch. Crisscross your lawn several times with the dethatcher, which will tear up most of the bad vegetation and expose your soil to the new seeds. Then seed and water as you would with a new lawn.

If you have only a few patches of lawn that need work, use a rake, or even a shovel, to prepare the ground, then seed and water. Cover those patches with about 1/4 inch of dirt or sand to keep the seeds in place. If you are seeding small areas, cover the seeded soil with burlap. Dampen the burlap daily. Seeds don't need light to germinate; they need warmth and humidity. The soil is already warm from the summer sun and the damp burlap will produce moisture. Using this method, seeds will germinate in about half the normal time.

Another solution is to simply "plug" the lawn. If you want zoysia grass, for instance, you can purchase little "sprigs" that are planted in furrowed rows 6 to 12 inches apart. Keep it watered, and in a few years it will fill in the gaps. There are a few problems with zoysia. It's invasive, it doesn't like shade at all and it turns a tan color from October to May.

LAWN THINGS TO DO IN AUGUST:

Mow your grass a little higher to protect it from the heat.

Make a daily inspection of the lawn looking for grub or beetle damage.

By now your lawn-mower blade is probably very dull; get it sharpened. Keep the underside of the mower clean so it will properly cut and "toss out" the grass.

GARDEN TIPS
EARLY

It's normal for tomatoes to stop producing when the temperature rises into the 90s and stays there. It's just so doggone hot in these "dog days" that the pollen gums up and becomes infertile. Keep watering and applying fungicides and insecticides. There will be more tomatoes later.

Powdery mildew and August often go hand in glove, or mildew on leaf, as the case may be. Mildew is the powdery, grayish white stuff you see on dahlias, honeysuckle, lilacs, privet, roses and zinnias. It arrives in August because it often overwinters in the Deep South, and its spores are blown northward every spring and summer.

Mildew thrives on evenings with heavy dew. To fight it, soak the soil when watering rather than sprinkling the foliage. Then buy a mildew fungicide containing sulfur. Benlate is a good one, but it must be used every 10 to 14 days. It can't save what's been infected, but it can protect what's left.

One year while mowing around the garden I saw a cantaloupe wobbling along the plant leaves. I thought the heat of the day was getting to me. I tiptoed up to the quaking melon . . . and there, sticking out from the far side of the melon, was the back end of a well-fed box turtle.

From then on I placed the melons on top of old flower pots as they neared maturity, and that seemed to eliminate the problem.

Also remember this: Cantaloupe vines have shallow roots and should be cultivated with care. Lifting the vines unnecessarily — except when charging box turtles are around — may reduce production by interfering with pollination.

By now you've probably logged about 10,000 foot miles behind the trusty lawn mower. It may be time to sharpen the blade again and change the oil. Also, try cutting the yard in different patterns for the rest of the summer. It will help break the monotony, and it's better for the grass if you cut it at different angles and from different directions. You'll get a whole new perspective on life, come up with a great idea and make $10 million. Just send me 10 percent.

We've talked about the importance of regular watering, but if you still need help, here's a formula I've found that will help you decide how much water you need:

If your garden hose is 1/2 inch in diameter, let the water run for about an hour to get the equivalent of one inch of rain. If your hose is 5/8 inch, let it run 37 minutes. If your hose is 3/4 inch, it will take only 24 minutes.

The type of sprinkler you use, of course, is a factor in this. To double-check, place a can under the spray and watch the clock. When there's an inch of water in the can, you'll know how long the sprinkler should run.

A man called me one day in August to report the strangest sight he had ever seen; a stalk had emerged from the ground near his house and on top of it was a large clump of lily-like flowers.

"What," he asked, "is that?"

The answer is the "magic lily," the "resurrection lily," or, more interestingly, the "naked lady." The plant is actually an amaryllis that emerges from bulbs that should be planted in the fall.

The man who called had forgotten that the heavy, straplike green leaves that emerged early in the spring and died back were also part of the plant's growth cycle. That leafy orchestra was the first announcement of the plant to come.

Magic lilies will do well in full sun or partial shade. They are extremely hardy and reproduce readily. They should be planted five inches deep and eight inches apart. After the blooms are gone, snip off the buds and fertilize.

As we near the end of the gardening season, it's essential to remove all old and rotting fruit from your garden. It provides the perfect nursery for next year's crop of insects and disease. Keep your garden clean as you go, and it will make the big, year-end cleanup much easier. It also keeps more crops coming this season.

Watch your late-summer beans for a disease called rust, which often makes its first appearance as we head toward Labor Day. It is found most commonly on mature beans having a dense canopy. Look for reddish-brown spots on lower leaf surfaces and pods. It's spread by wind and with garden tools. Fungicides like Maneb or sulfur dust will keep it under control. Begin spraying soon.

Discontinue spraying your fruit trees two weeks before harvest to avoid having poisonous residue on the food. Be sure to check the pesticide or fungicide labels for specific intervals while you are spraying.

Now is the time to begin transforming your luffa gourd into what the pioneers used it for — a sponge. The luffa is a gourd that grows almost two feet in length. It can be eaten like a zucchini or cucumber when young, but as it matures its color turns from green to yellow which means it's ready to pick.

First, soak the gourd in water until the skin peels away and a fibrous skeleton is left—that's the sponge. Remove the seeds for next year's crop and let the sponge dry in the sun for a day. After it has cured, wash it thoroughly and take it to the kitchen. You'll find it is very stiff and coarse, but it will make an excellent pot-scrubber and conversation piece.

In Japan luffas are used for shoe soles, filters and pillow stuffings. In Europe they are used in health spas and for bathing. I tried that once and didn't like it. It was like bathing with a scouring pad.

It's still not too late to begin a fall garden of warm-weather crops, including bush beans, carrots, beets and transplants of cabbage, cauliflower and broccoli — if you can find them. It's a little early yet to plant lettuce, mustard greens, spinach and turnips in a fall garden. They don't like the heat. Late August or early September is a better time for them.

One of the best ways to protect your garden from winter erosion — and to add mulch at the same time — is to plant a "green manure" in the later summer or fall.

That means after the vegetables have all been picked and the garden has been cleaned out, you want to plant a cover crop of rye to protect the area. You want to sow about 1/3 of a pound per 100 square feet. If you still have some late crops, sow the rye between the rows. Fertilize carefully, either by broadcasting or sidedressing along the rows.

In the spring plow the rye under a little while before you plant the garden.

The prime value of this "green manure" is to add organic matter to the soil. But because the decaying process "steals" some nitrogen from the ground, you'll want to add a little extra nitrogen in the spring.

MIDDLE

The peace and tranquillity of good night's sleep in mid-August was broken a few years ago by the sound of the telephone ringing. The caller was excited.

"My plant," she said. "You must come see it."

"At midnight?" I said. "Can't it wait until morning?"

But I knew the answer was no, because her plant was the night-blooming cereus. It's an usual member of the cactus family, with broad, leathery leaves that narrow to a point at the top.

Once a year, usually in midsummer, older cereus plants put out magnificent, water-lilylike flowers; white with purple on the outer petals. To get one to bloom, you need porous, well-drained

soil and eternal vigilance with the water; the plant must be kept moist all summer. It needs soil on the dry side in winter, with a bright location and temperatures at 40 to 45 degrees.

Is the night-blooming cereus rare? Not judging by the number of late-blooming phone calls I get.

So if you have one and it's getting ready to bloom, do me a favor; don't call me, I'll call you.

Given the hot weather in mid to late August, you may be tempted to fertilize your droopy looking trees and shrubs to pep them up. DON'T do it. A belt of fertilizer now could stimulate growth that won't have time to harden off by winter and will probably be killed by cold weather. You don't want to fertilize again until late in the fall, after the first freeze has stopped growth or the leaves have dropped. Fertilizer then will help the tree roots get ready for next year.

Your grapes have changed color by now, either to red, or purple, or possibly a different shade of green than they were initially. But most cultivars shouldn't be harvested until two to three weeks after the color change to give them time to fully ripen. The grapes may look ready to eat before then, but they are not.

It's time to begin searching the catalogs for the tulip, daffodil, crocus and other bulbs you'll want blooming in your garden next spring. But it's way too early to plant them now. If you did, they could sprout prematurely in the warm weather, using up all the gusto they need for next spring. Look over the catalogs and order now, but be patient; most bulb companies don't ship until planting time anyway.

While you're waiting, draw a map of exactly where you want each bulb. Be creative. Have fun. You might even work the soil and add a little fertilizer to get it ready.

If you haven't done it yet, be sure to prune and destroy all the raspberry and blackberry canes that bore fruit this year. They will not produce fruit again but could produce disease. It helps to thin out the patch, and you can get an idea of what you'll have next year by seeing what's left.

It's time to take cuttings from annuals such as impatiens, coleus, geraniums and wax begonias to start some plants that will overwinter indoors. Be sure to pick new, healthy growth. Use sharp shears. Use a root fertilizer and place the cuttings in vermiculite, perlite or peat moss rather than water. Keep them moist and in bright, indirect light while they get started. They need the very best treatment this time of year.

From our Where Have You Heard This Before Dept. comes another reminder: Keep picking the buds off the bedding plants to keep them flowering. Keep removing the crops from the garden to keep the plants producing. It's too easy to neglect all that in the heat of August. If they look too sickly, trim off all the tops. Most will rejuvenate for a fall show.

LATE

If you're lucky enough to have a pear tree, remember that pears ripen best off the tree. Harvest them when the fruit turns from a dark green to a lighter green but before they get to an over-ripe, screaming yellow. Set the pears in a cool, dry, brightly lit place, and they'll be edible in just a few days.

Continue to hand-pick bagworms and look for or any tent caterpillars that might have set up homemaking in the crotches of your trees. You may need shears to cut out the homes of the caterpillars. Their nests can be burned, or you can kill the pests with Sevin, provided you tear a hole in the bag first. Be sure to hunt them late in the day when all the caterpillars have crawled back into their tents.

One of the most reliable methods of improving poor garden soil is to plant a "green-manure" cover crop. This adds organic matter to the soil and, depending on the cover crop used, it also helps add nitrogen to the soil.

The type of "cover crop" you should consider includes hairy vetch, burr clover, soybeans, cowpeas and sorghums.

Most cover crops are legumes; that is, their roots have nitrogen-fixing nodules that extract nitrogen from the air and put it in the soil. You should sow the green-manure crop in early fall, let it grow into the winter, then plow it under four to eight weeks before you are ready to plant.

If your winter squash is ready to pick now, you planted it too soon. You want to harvest winter squash about Oct. 1. The flavor is usually better then because cold weather increases the sugar content.

If they must be picked now — and most green winter squash varieties are ready when they get some strong brown, yellow or bronze color to them — cure them in the sun and store them where it's 55 to 60 degrees.

But if you had planted them about July 1, you wouldn't have this problem. It's summer squash, like zucchini, that should be planted in May.

I saw a cartoon recently that showed a family returning from vacation. A small boy got out of the car and was standing in grass over his head. He turned to his father and said, "Hey, Dad, you forgot to turn off the grass."

Alas, the grass doesn't turn off. Before leaving for vacation, even in August, be sure that someone will cut the lawn. It's better for the grass and provides more security for your home.

Don't do any heavy pruning of landscape plants now. They are getting ready for winter and don't need any ends exposed. It could lead to death from a cold. When winter gets here you can prune some hollies, magnolias or evergreens for Christmas foliage, but do it carefully because those cuttings will leave a "hole" in the plant.

It's especially important that you keep your evergreen trees, azaleas and rhododendrons well-watered in the fall in order to get them through the winter. They often have shallow roots and are more susceptible to drying out than other trees.

FRED'S TIPS

Most insecticides contain a substance that helps them stick to the plants in the rain. If you get an inch or more of rain, however, chances are the insecticide has been washed away. But that still doesn't mean the food is safe to eat. Always observe the time listed on the chemical that specifies the days between application and harvest. You'll have to reapply after a heavy rain.

Fall webworms are those green or yellow insects that spin a web over the ends of branches and turn the leaves inside into skeletons. The web is then extended to take in fresh foliage. The webs can be cut off and burned, or the webworms can be killed with Sevin or Malathion, but you must open the bag for the spray to penetrate.

Webworms are often confused with tent caterpillars, which usually live in the crotches of trees. Some webworms particularly like flowering crabs.

The age-old way of preserving herbs is to dry them by hanging the bouquets in a well-ventilated, dust-free room. If the air is dusty, or if the herbs have seeds that may fall, the herbs can be hung in bunches in brown paper bags. Just be sure the bag has a lot of holes punched in it for ventilation.

But a newer way to preserve herbs is to freeze them. First wash the herbs, pat off the excess water, place them in plastic bags and pop them into the freezer as soon as possible. Mint tarragon, lovage, parsley, chives, sorrel and sweet marjoram can be handled this way. You can just snip off what you need from the frozen herbs.

Another method, according to the U.S. Department of Agriculture, is to put chopped herbs into an ice-cube tray, fill with water and freeze. Store the cubes in a plastic bag and drop them into stews or soups as needed.

Rosemary is a tender herb that can be preserved for the winter by taking a baby plant indoors. It's done by a process called "layering." Take a sharp knife and partially cut through the stem of a rosemary plant where it's still covered with soil. After a few weeks, roots will form at the cut. Then cut the whole rooted shoot from the mother plant and put it in a new pot. Take it indoors, but give it bright light all winter — possibly even adding fluorescent light during the short winter days. It can go back outdoors next spring.

I'm always collecting garden ideas from people who listen to my radio or television shows, and here's one to protect grapes from the birds: Use old nylon stockings. Just pull the stockings over your grape bunches and tie both ends. The stockings will expand as the grapes grow, you'll keep the bunches intact, and you can reuse the stockings next year.

Did you know you can use the berries of the pyracantha to make a delicious, orange-colored jelly? The bush, which does have long, sharp needles to protect its crop, bears fruit in late summer.

According to one Purdue University horticulturist, you make the jelly by adding one cup of water to each pound of well washed berries. Boil the water 20 to 25 minutes.

Drain the mixture into a flannel bag and press out the juice, since that's what you need for the jelly. Mix seven cups of water to three cups of pyracantha juice and add the juice of two lemons. Bring the mixture to a boil and add jelling agent. Pour into sterilized jars and seal with paraffin. Then pop some bread in the toaster next Saturday morning and spread on the jelly.

Here's a tip that may help save a tree that's already been damaged in a heavy windstorm. If a heavy limb has been injured to the extent that it must be removed with a chain saw, make your first cut underneath the limb at the point where the branch meets the bark of the trunk.

Cut through the bark with an upward stroke about 1 inch deep. If you saw through the limb from the top without making the undercut first, there is a good chance the heavy branch will rip the bark off the limb as it falls.

Never leave a stub of the limb on the tree. Cut it off almost flush with the trunk. A stub will only serve as an entry point for insects and disease. Do not use a wound dressing on the cut. If you do, no air can get to the wound, and it will fester.

FRED'S SUPER TIP

If this summer is typical of the rest, you are now locked in mortal combat with the dreaded Japanese beetle. The odd thing about the beetles is they are spotty; they'll hit one neighborhood hard one year, another the next year.

We've already discussed some prevention methods in a previous chapter. The very best method — although it can be monumentally time-consuming — is to go out early in the morning or evening when they are the most sluggish, pick them off and dispose of them. Failing that, Sevin or Orthene are the best chemical controls. Japanese beetle "traps" are also available, but they may just lure more bugs into your yard then you might ordinarily have.

The Japanese beetle is a tough foe — and getting tougher. It will help you to defeat it if you know and understand its life cycle. So here, courtesy of the University of Kentucky, is your Japanese beetle primer.

History — The bugs were first found in the United States in 1916 near Riverton, N.J., probably hauled into this country in the grub stage hitchhiking

on some imported nursery stock. Until this time the beetle was known only in Japan, where it is not a major pest.

But it soon found a home in the states; there were hundreds of new plants to feed on and no effective natural enemies. It eventually made its way to Kentucky in 1937, where about 30 acres were found infested on the southern edge of Louisville. That infestation was ended with a pesticide, but the problem was too big; the beetles kept on coming.

Habits — The adult beetles emerge fror the ground and begin feeding on plants — and they feed on about 300 plants from roses to poison ivy — in June. The individual beetle lives about 30 to 45 days. They feed in groups, starting at the top of a plant and working down to its toes, much preferring exposed, direct sun light. A single beetle doesn't eat much, but in packs they are sheer terrors.

The beetles like tender foliage, chewing out the tissue between the veins of the leaf, leaving it classically "skeletonized." Odor seems to be a big factor in which plants they select, and they generally leave the thicker, tougher leaves alone.

They spread mostly by flight. An adult can fly 5 miles, but a mile or two is more common; they always seem to find enough to eat in that distance.

Life cycle — The adults lay eggs as soon as they emerge from the ground and mate. The females leave the plants in the afternoon, burrow 2 to 4 inches in the soil and lay eggs. They are very careful mothers, laying one to four eggs every three to four days for several weeks — about 40 to 60 in total.

After hatching, the beetles will spend about 10 months of the year in the soil as a white grub. They feed on the roots of living plants and grass. While late-summer rains are needed to keep eggs and newly hatched grubs from drying out, the grubs will burrow a few inches deeper into the soil during drought conditions. Most, however, rarely move more than 30 inches in any one direction from the place where they hatched.

The beetles overwinter in this grub stage, sometimes digging 8 to 10 inches into the soil to protect themselves. They become inactive when the soil temperature hits 50 degrees. In the spring, when the ground warms above 50, they move up again. Following a short feeding period they pupate in an earthen shell, turn into beetles and emerge as hungry, flying beetles ready to consume your roses, hardy hibiscus and larches, et al.

Natural controls — Many birds, including bobwhites, cardinals, robins, crows and grackles, eat Japanese beetles — and isn't it nice to know grackles are good for something? Also starlings, grackles and crows will eat the grubs in heavily infested areas; a large flock on your lawn is a sign of grub problems. Moles, skunks and shrews also eat them, but tear up your lawn while doing it.

Another "organic" approach is "milky spore disease," a commercial product that may help reduce the number of grubs in your lawn, although the beetles may just fly over from your neighbor's yard and begin again.

September

✐ September Checklist

LAWN TIPS

☐ Give your lawn an application of high-nitrogen fertilizer.

☐ It's time to chemically control broadleaf weeds.

☐ You still have time to rebuild or renovate your lawn.

EARLY

☐ Get Christmas cactuses ready to bloom.

☐ Plant container-grown or balled and burlapped trees and shrubs.

☐ Bring houseplants indoors.

☐ Check damage done to trees and shrubs by lawn mower.

☐ Remove old raspberry canes and clean up under apple trees.

☐ Divide day lilies, iris, phlox and peonies.

☐ Fertilize strawberries.

☐ Plant parsley seeds for indoor growing.

☐ Plant turnip seeds.

☐ Dust lilacs, zinnias and phlox for powdery mildew; rake leaves

☐ Take cuttings of impatiens, begonias, coleus and geraniums

☐ Dig potatoes.

MIDDLE

☐ Spray roses for diseases and insects.

☐ Have soil analysis done.

☐ Store leftover vegetable and flower seeds.

☐ Dig up and store tubers and corms from tuberous begonias, gladioluses, dahlias, cannas, caladiums and geraniums.

☐ Pick heads off annual flowers to keep them blooming.

☐ Reduce water and stop fertilizing houseplants.

☐ Plant spring-flowering bulbs in pots for early blooming next season.

☐ Gather dirt and mulch to prepare for mounding around rose plants.

☐ Water trees and shrubs.

☐ Begin harvesting gourds.

☐ Harvest flowers for indoor display.

☐ Divide and replant clumps of hollyhocks, perennial salvia and primroses; also transplant columbine, lenten roses and wallflowers.

☐ Water azaleas, rhododendron and camellias.

☐ Transplant poppies.

☐ Start a fall salad garden.

LATE

☐ Plant gooseberries.

☐ Harvest popcorn before first frost.

☐ Prepare garden area or raised bed for spring pea plantings.

☐ Begin preparing poinsettias for putting out red bracts.

SUPER TIP

☐ Indoor plant cuttings.

September, with its clean nights and bright, sunny mornings, is the reward we've earned for living around here in July and August. It's the time when the world wakes from its late summer slumber to the fresh breezes of autumn and realizes, "Holy cow, I've got to transplant my iris and sow some more grass seed!"

September comes from the Latin word *septem*, meaning "seven." Never mind that it's the ninth month. You should know your Romans better than that. September was the seventh month, but by the time Julius Caesar was finished, it was in the ninth slot, and there it shall stay.

The average high temperature in Kentuckiana in September is 80.6 degrees. The average low is 59.1 degrees. The average precipitation is 3.35 inches. That's another nice thing about this country: Most months — spring to fall — average about one inch of rain a week.

The rainiest September since they started keeping records was in 1979, when 10.49 inches fell. The driest was September 1953, when .27 inches fell.

The hottest September day was Sept. 5, 1954, when it was 104 degrees. The coldest was 33 degrees on Sept. 30, 1949, which could have put a little frost on the pumpkin.

The longest drought in Louisville history ran from Sept. 29, 1924, to Oct. 30, 1924, a period of 32 days without rain. We hit 31 days in the summer of '88.

There are 13 hours and one minute of sun on Sept. 1, and 11 hours and 51 minutes of sun on Sept. 30, so get out the blankets. The average soil temperature ranges from 70 to 77 degrees.

Jesse James, an American desperado who knew some long green when he saw it, was born Sept. 5, 1847, and the Treaty of Paris, which officially ended the Revolutionary War in America, was signed Sept. 3, 1783.

LAWN TIPS

September is a great time to look at your lawn from the human perspective. Imagine that your front yard — or even your back yard — had won $25 million in Lotto America and had spent the entire summer indulging in frantic rounds of golf, volleyball, croquet, badminton and softball. By the time September got here, it was bent, battered and exhausted; barely able to pop up some new shoots, sorely in need of peace, quiet and replenishment.

It needs some refreshing, pick-me-up, high-nitrogen fertilizer such as a 27-3-6 at summer's end.

Just like the rest of us.

An average 4,000-square-foot lawn contains about 3 million grass plants, which is a lot of tired feet. So help it out. Prepare to fertilize now, in October, and some years even in November or December, weather permitting. Now is the best time because it will do the roots the most good; spring fertilization tends to promote heavy top growth at the expense of a good, anchoring root system.

The one ingredient your lawn lusts for this time of year is nitrogen, which helps restore its density and green color. The other items it needs in lesser amounts are phosphate and potash, also called potassium. Each of those items plays a vital part in lawn growth, but nitrogen is the key.

When you purchase fertilizer you will see that it is labeled with numbers such as 10-10-10 or 27-3-6. Those numbers refer to the percentage of nitrogen, phosphate and potash in the bag or bottle.

A 50-pound bag of 10-6-4 fertilizer, for instance, will be 10 percent nitrogen, 6 percent phosphate and 4 percent potash. That means the bag will have 5 pounds of nitrogen, 3 pounds of phosphate and 2 pounds of potash. The remaining 40 pounds in the bag is inert material — called filler or carrier — put in there to fill the bag and make you feel as if you got your money's worth.

Unless your soil test says otherwise, your soil shouldn't need a lot of phosphate or potash. You can even use some high-nitrogen fertilizers — such as ammonium nitrate (34-0-0), or even urea (45-0-0) — which are often available in farm-supply stores, and often at much cheaper prices than regular garden nurseries.

Failing that, the "special" high-nitrogen fertilizers you see in the nursery centers — such as 27-3-6 or 32-4-8 — are very good, especially the ones that are the "slow release" variety that lets the nitrogen sink more slowly into the soil. Also, these special fertilizers contain just enough phosphate and potash to keep your lawn happy. Continued use of them will keep the soil at just the right balance for many, many years.

But here is some VERY IMPORTANT INFORMATION: The special high-nitrogen fertilizers you find in nurseries have particles of uniform size, low "burn" potential and user-friendly instructions right on the bag.

Most of the farm-supply bags do not have detailed instructions, nor are those fertilizers particularly designed for home use. You may be spending more for the nursery fertilizers, but they are made for people who need some built-in protection against mistakes that can damage or even destroy a lawn. When in doubt, just buy the nursery product, read the instructions and use it.

The most common mistake most homeowners make is overfertilization; if 25 pounds of 32-4-8 is good, than 50 pounds must be terrific. The general rule of thumb for fertilization is 1 pound of "actual" nitrogen for each 1,000 square feet of lawn — which really isn't very much.

Depending on the nitrogen content and the type of spreader you use, you may only want from 2 to 4 pounds of fertilizer on a 1,000-square-foot area. It's tough to spread it that thinly without a little care and practice. But even using twice that amount can cause an excessive flush of growth — or even grass burn.

The University of Kentucky recommends that applications of high-nitrogen fertilizer should be made every four to six weeks during fall and early winter, with two or three applications best for the average lawn.

The push-type spreaders are the very best to guarantee uniform distribution. It will take a little time to adjust the calibration to the exact amount of fertilizer you want to spread — and even the size of the fertilizer granule will vary from company to company. As a public service, estimated calibrations are often fixed to the spreaders — and even the bags of fertilizer. But any caring homeowner should invest in a spreader — or perhaps split the cost with a couple of neighbors since spreaders are only needed a few days a year.

There are other methods of spreading fertilizer too. A "broadcast" spreader is often quicker and simpler, but may not offer the precise distribution since the granules are often flying 15 to 25 feet.

You can also buy "liquid" lawn fertilizers — the same rules and ratios of nitrogen, phosphate and potash apply — that can be attached to your garden hose for easy application. Those types of spreaders are particularly good for people with small lawns and patio gardens or who don't want fertilizer granules all over their sidewalk, carport or patio.

No matter what type of granular spreader you use, it's very important that you wash it clean, dry it well and coat all moving parts with oil after every use. If you don't — and thousands of spreaders suffer from this painful death every year — the high salt content of the fertilizers will cause rust. Also, never wash fertilizer from the spreader onto the lawn; it could cause uneven growth or excessive burning.

If your soil test indicates your soil is on the acid side, it might require an application of lime to "sweeten it" just a little, a process that facilitates better grass growth. Homeowners can find bagged limestone pellets at many garden centers. It can also be applied with a good spreader.

BROADLEAF WEEDS — September is also the best time to try to kill many of the broadleaf weeds such as chickweed, dandelions and plaintain. I recommend a mixture of 2,4-D, MCPP or Banvil to do the job. They are readily available in garden centers. One problem you might have is that these herbicides often need some rain or irrigation to work, and September and October are often the driest months. So you may need to water the lawn to help them work.

GARDEN TIPS
EARLY

Start preparing your Christmas cactuses to bloom by giving them 12 hours of complete darkness and night temperatures no higher than 70 degrees. Cover the plants with a thick bag or cloth, but be careful not to injure the stems. Be sure they receive some indirect sunlight the other 12 hours. Do this for eight weeks to 10 weeks, and the buds will appear.

If you don't want to do all that, constant temperatures of about 55 degrees at night will also stimulate the plants to bloom, but it's not easy to find those temperatures in early September.

Fall is an excellent time to plant many container-grown trees or shrubs or nursery stock that has been balled and wrapped in burlap. Planting bare-root stock during this season is a risky venture because the roots do not have a lot of time to "dig in" before Old Man Winter arrives. You can plant bare-root stock after a couple of hard frosts.

Be sure to dig a hole at least twice as wide as the roots, plant at the same depth the tree or shrub grew in the nursery and water well. Stake the taller trees to keep them from rocking in the wind, or the roots will not settle. Be sure your ties don't cut into the tree. Old hose with wire strung through it works well.

Don't forget to bring in houseplants that were moved outdoors for the summer, especially when the temperature consistently falls below 55 degrees. Gradually decrease the amount of light to keep leaf drop to a minimum. Check for disease and bugs who might want to winter indoors before placing the plants next to other houseplants.

Now that we're easing into the end of the lawn-mower season, take a walk around your lawn and inspect trees and shrubs for lawn-mower "teeth marks" that are often the result of careless mowing.

Good watering and an application of fertilizer after the first frost will help the tree or shrub regain its strength. While you're looking, don't be alarmed if you white pines or arborvitaes are browning off in the center and dropping some of their needles. All evergreens shed needles at some time but not all at once as do deciduous varieties.

If you haven't removed the old raspberry canes that bore fruit, you better get moving. All suckers outside the hills and rows should be removed. Be sure to clean up all the fallen fruit and leaves around the apple trees while you're at it. It keeps down the disease.

You still have time to transplant or divide day lilies, iris, phlox and peonies. But remember, peonies don't especially like to be moved and are willing to bloom for 30 to 40 years in the same place if you keep them properly fed and pruned.

Be sure to apply two pounds of ammonium nitrate per 100 square feet of strawberry bed area. Brush the granules off the leaves to avoid damage and water right away. All this will put strawberries in your ice cream next year.

Parsley is a fun and useful herb to grow indoors in the winter, and planting can begin now. I think the key to getting parsley seeds jump-started is to soak them eight to 12 hours in water before planting. After the bath, plant the seeds in a six-inch pot of good soil. Keep them in good light and thin out the seedlings to three sturdy plants. Mist occasionally along with regular watering.

When you harvest parsley for garnishes, salads and soups, cut only the outer leaves so the inner ones can develop.

What is the 15th most popular vegetable and the fourth most valuable in terms of nutrition? Why, of course, it's the turnip!

Turnips are one of the better fall crops. They withstand cold temperatures and can be harvested until the ground freezes. They can be eaten raw or cooked and eaten like potatoes. So plant some now. Broadcast the seeds over a wide area, and as they emerge from the soil, pull some of the younger plants and use the "greens" in a salad. They're great.

When looking around some of the gardens in our area in early September, I often see the leaves of plants like lilacs, zinnias and phlox covered with powdery mildew, a grayish substance. University of Kentucky horticulturists recommend dusting with sulfur, and I've also had good luck with Benlate or Denomyl.

Rake up and destroy the leaves at season's end, and next season leave a little more space around the plants, which will improve air circulation and cut down on disease.

There's still time to take cuttings of impatiens, begonias, coleus and geraniums for next year. Be sure to cut three to six inches from the healthiest plants for better rooting indoors.

Potatoes can be dug before the skins are tough; they almost melt in your mouth at that stage. But if you want potatoes to keep, it's best to wait until the vines have been dead for about two weeks, which is often this time of year.

Avoid digging potatoes in bright sun and don't bruise them. Potatoes can be stored for four to six months, but it takes a temperature of about 40 degrees, high humidity and proper ventilation to keep them.

Although it's much easier just to buy new trees at a nursery, you might find it interesting one year to try to grow a tree from seeds. Obviously, some trees are easier to raise than others; all you have to do is look around maple trees for the "youngsters" that have seeded themselves to see how prolific they are.

It's also important to remember that the trees found in nurseries are often grown from cuttings or graftings of the very best trees, thus almost guaranteeing the "baby" will have all the right characteristics. A tree grown from seed may not have all the best characteristics of its parents — much like a human child isn't always a carbon copy of his parents.

That said, however, maybe you'd still like to plant the seeds of a favorite tree

— perhaps even a favorite dogwood. Here's how.

Just as soon as dogwood berries turn bright red in the early fall, harvest a handful. Timing is the key here, because the birds or squirrels might beat you to it.

Peel the fleshy, red pulp from each berry, exposing the hard, yellowish seed. Place the seeds is a small glass jar or plastic freezer bag and store them in the refrigerator for three months. That's important because the seeds must go through some physiological maturation that's induced by the cold, and the refrigerator duplicates that.

At the end of the chill period, sow the seeds 1/2 inch deep in a seed flat filled with moist, seed-starting soil mix. Provide bottom heat of about 70 degrees, and the seeds should germinate in several weeks. Give the seedlings bright light and feed every two weeks with water-soluble 20-20-20 fertilizer diluted to half-strength.

When the seedlings are about 2 inches high, transplant them to individual 4-inch pots. As soon as the roots have filled the pots, transplant them into your garden. But be sure to wait until the last late-spring frost date has ended.

With dogwoods it will take several years for them to bloom but it's well worth the wait. If you do other trees, the germination period may be 3 or 4 months. Maintaining high humidity and high moisture the whole time is critical to the process.

MIDDLE

Don't neglect your roses. Keep up a regular spray schedule for diseases and insects. Roses need a lot more care later in the season, but for now constant surveillance is what's needed.

Place leftover vegetable and flower seeds in tightly sealed jars and store them in a dark, cool, dry place. Many seeds will keep for years, and since manufacturers insist on placing a 10-year supply in some packages, you can save a lot of money.

It's getting close to the time to dig your tuberous begonias, glads, dahlias and cannas, although cannas often bloom gloriously into October when all else is fading.

Gladiolus corms should be dug when the leaves have begun to turn yellow. Caladiums, geraniums and tuberous begonias should be dug before a killing frost. You can digs cannas and dahlias after a light frost, but a heavy frost can kill them because it seeps into their roots.

After digging them up, remove the foliage, leaving a short stub, and let the corms and tubers dry for several days. Store them in dry sand or peat moss in a cool, dry place where they won't freeze. A dusting of fungicide will help, but check them all winter; throw out any that show signs of mold or decay.

Keep picking the heads off your annual flowers. Many will have a sudden revival in the shorter, cooler days of summer and will surprise you with lovely blooms until frost.

Because your indoor plants have to get ready to snooze through the winter, you should water them less frequently and stop fertilizing them. Everybody needs a rest some time.

Although it's only September, now is the best time to plant some spring-flowering bulbs in pots so you can force them to bloom indoors in December and January.

It's easy to do. Plant two or three prime daffodil or tulip bulbs in a pot with their tips just above the soil, moisten the soil a little and place the pot in a refrigerator for 10 to 13 weeks. The bulbs will not bloom unless they're fooled into thinking it's winter and the milk is actually a snowman.

When time is up, place the pot in a cool, sunny location and allow three to four weeks for blooms. It will help spring come faster.

It's too early to mound protective dirt around your rose plants; that shouldn't be done until after the leaves drop and the ground is almost frozen. But you should have the dirt, or whatever you'll use for protection, in place and ready to go. It's no fun to move in cold weather. Don't fertilize your roses anymore; give them time to harden off before the snow hits.

Keep watering the baby trees and shrubs you planted this year but don't fertilize them. Surveys have shown that water in the fall is vital to having healthy trees in the spring. It's especially vital following summers with long droughts.

Check your gourds to see if the stems are brown and have begun to dry. If they have, it's time to harvest. Use a sharp knife or shears, leaving a few inches of stem to avoid bruising the fruit. Gourds should be cured for two weeks in 70- to 80-degree heat to preserve them.

Pumpkins and winter squash can be picked when the rind is hard and fully colored. If you can easily dent the rind with a fingernail, they're not ready. They should be stored in a cool place, or they'll be a pulpy mess before you can carve the first jack-o'-lantern.

Now is the time to harvest flowers such as strawflowers, statice, baby's breath and cockscomb for indoor display. After cutting, hang them upside down in a dry, well-ventilated area to help preserve them.

Although your perennial garden may have almost finished blooming for the year, you can get a good start on next year by dividing and replanting over-crowded clumps of hollyhocks, perennial salvia and primroses.

Also, check your columbine, lenten roses and wallflowers for seedlings that may have come up during the summer. If they are too crowded, transplant seedlings to another location. Columbine can take over an entire area.

Don't forget to water azaleas, rhododendron and camellias. This is a critical time for their newly formed flower buds. Very often azaleas don't bloom in the spring because of improper watering the previous fall.

Late summer to early fall is also the best time to transplant your poppies, which should have begun to peep back through the soil after resting from their spring performance. Many varieties like a coarse soil. They can be difficult to transplant, but once they find a home, they will cheerfully bloom for decades.

Remember, it's not too late to start a fall salad garden. Lettuce, spinach, mustard greens, radishes, onions and kale often do better in cool fall weather. Just a few square feet of garden space will give you fresh vegetables into October. Be sure to spray with a fungicide such as Maneb or Zineb; fungus is a real problem in the humid fall weather.

LATE

I remember my grandmother picking gooseberries for gooseberry pie, and with some care you can have them too.

Plant gooseberries in the fall, spacing plants about five feet apart, and setting them two to three inches deeper than they were growing when purchased.

Immediately after planting, cut all canes to six to eight inches above ground level. The first winter after planting, cut all but the six strongest canes back to ground level. Thereafter, prune each winter, cutting out the three oldest canes and all but three of the new season's growth. With this system, each of the plants will bear fruit on one-, two- or three-year-old canes, producing a maximum crop.

Gooseberries need regular fertilizing. In late winter feed a tablespoon of potassium sulfate per square yard. In early spring add a tablespoon of ammonium sulfate per square yard. Every three years add two tablespoons of superphosphate every square yard.

Start picking when the berries are pea-sized and use the larger berries that follow for pies just like Grandma used to bake.

If you grew popcorn this year, you must pick it before the first frosts, which often occur in early October. If you wait too long, frost will cause mold on the ears.

At harvest, the moisture level for most popcorn will be about 16 percent. The best popping moisture is about 13.5 percent. To dry the corn, the husks should be removed and the ears hung to dry in a warm, well-ventilated area. After two to three weeks, toss some kernels into a popper and check to see if all of them pop.

If not, wait a week and try again. The popcorn is ready when all of the kernels pop. There are a lot worse ways of doing research.

Store the kernels in an airtight container. They can last years if kept cool or frozen.

It's not too soon to prepare a garden area — maybe even a raised bed — for next year's pea plantings. Peas can be planted as early as March and preparing the ground now can make it easier. With a small raised bed, you'll be able to cover the area with clear plastic, getting a big jump on the season.

If you want your poinsettias to put out red bracts in time for Christmas, begin placing them in total darkness for 15 hours a day from very late September to early October. Keep them in bright light the other nine hours of the day.

Some people use paper bags pulled well down over the plant; others go as far as putting the plants in a closet. It is important that the darkness be total; even a few hours of light in that 15-hour period can prevent the bracts from co-operating. It usually takes eight to 10 weeks for the bracts to show red. After that, normal care will carry the plants to Christmas.

If you keep the poinsettias in a cool place with indirect light, they will stay healthy for many weeks after Christmas.

FRED'S TIPS

Gardening season may be almost over, but that doesn't mean there's not some pesticides left in their containers in the garage. They can be saved, and here's the best way to do it:

Store them in a locked room or cabinet where children can't get close to them. Don't store them near feed, seed or garden clothing. Store them in well-lighted, ventilated areas that will not freeze. Store them in their original containers and mark the purchase date on the sides of the containers so you'll know their age. Keep an up-to-date inventory.

Although spring is usually the biggest sales period for mail-order nurseries, we still order many plants for the fall season. So here are some tips to help avoiding ordering problems.

To help people determine if a particular tree or plant can survive the local winters, the continental United States is divided into "hardness zones," with northern Wisconsin being a "3" and the southern tip of Florida a "10." Indiana and Kentucky fall into zones 5, 6 and 7. To be sure your plants will survive even the toughest Kentucky winters, order plants that are hardy in zone 5, which means they should survive temperatures of 20 degrees below zero.

Don't be misled by fantastic claims. Trees that grow 20 feet year — and that is virtually impossible outside of Brazil — are usually very brittle and susceptible to ice and wind damage.

If you have any doubts about a product, contact your local agriculture agents. They are well-trained people and can save you a lot of money.

When the pumpkins in your garden are full-sized but not fully hardened, let your children and their friends pick out their pumpkins and inscribe their names on them. Use a nail or small screwdriver but don't write too deeply. As the pumpkins mature, the names will harden into the rind.

If you really feel ambitious, you might have them write a poem, a message, or even the Gettysburg Address.

Keep checking your pets for fleas, which are a real problem this time of year. Use flea collars, give them regular baths with flea powder and check the furniture for evidence that the pests have moved inside, often with your pet as the moving service.

Be wary of any advertisements claiming that ultrasonic sound devices can scare insects from your yard or house. Research done by the U.S. Department of Agriculture show they don't work, especially the ones that are supposed to stop mosquitoes from biting. Stick with repellents, screens and fly swatters.

Not all plant problems stem from improper environment or attacks of pests and diseases. All houseplants eventually die from having lived long, happy lives.

The popular piggyback plant is a case in point. No matter how well you care for it, eventually the time comes when it is spent and must be discarded — but not before you have rooted some of the baby plants that began life on top of the old leaves, hence the name piggyback.

To propagate the piggyback, clip the mature leaf and the accompanying smaller plant, set it on the soil surface, secure with a bobby pin and water. After the plantlet forms its own roots, the old "mother leaf" will wither away.

Tree-stump removal is a problem that haunts many gardeners, especially after a bad spell of summer thunderstorms. There are professionals with big grinding machines that can crunch the stump down below the level of your lawnmower blade, but they can be very expensive.

You can also buy little cans of "stump decay" products in hardware stores or nurseries, but that can also be expensive. If you've got the time, energy and tools, you can dig out the stumps. An easier solution might be to drill holes in the stump with a large wood bit, then fill the holes with fertilizer. This encourages decay, but it still may be years before the stump disappears.

Contrary to what many people believe, fall fertilizing with slow-release nitrogen can help reduce winter injury to broadleaf and narrow-leafed evergreens and improve spring growth. But — and this is a BIG but — do not apply the fertilizer until after the first killing frost. You do not want to encourage late plant growth.

Protect young, thin-barked trees against frost cracks by wrapping the trunks with protective paper or strips of burlap. Apple, ash, beech, elm, linden, London plane, maple, oak, poplar, tulip tree, walnut and willow are susceptible to cracking.

People often ask me about large, green worms on tomato plants. The worms are bad enough, but what's really strange-looking are those white spiny objects on their backs.

The big worm is the tomato hornworm, and I never use an insecticide on him; he's so big I just pick him off. The white objects are cocoons of a parasitic wasp — the braconid. It lays its eggs on the back of the hornworm and as the young emerge they eat the hornworm. It's not a pleasant thought, but those wasps are just part of the mostly unseen insect world that gets us through a season.

A Purdue entomologist recently warned that yellow-jacket nests can be hazardous to the health of people living nearby, and eradication should only be tried at night when the swarming insects have returned home. There are "long-range" sprays available, but John McDonald advised homeowners to get professional extermination help for any nests found inside buildings.

Cut the heads from your sunflower stalks just as the seeds begin to turn brown and the backs of the heads turn yellow. Hang them upside down in a warm, dry place, like a garage rafter or the attic. Basements are too humid for storage this time of year.

Let the heads hang for about three weeks before removing the seeds. If the seeds start to fall earlier, place paper bags around the heads. Just for the record, the tallest sunflower ever recorded was 17 feet, 3 inches. The widest known head was 33 1/4 inches.

One of the methods I've heard to keep deer out of your pasture, yard or garden is to hang Dial soap around the place. Even if it doesn't work, you'll have clean mosquitoes.

Think about using gourds around the house as fall and winter decorations. If you didn't raise any, you can often find them at farmer's markets. Dry them well and wax or shellack them for more shine.

If your azaleas are looking a little on the pale green side, the problem could be an iron deficiency called chlorosis. To correct the problem, treat the plants with chelated iron or iron sulfate. Spray it directly onto the leaf surface or soak the soil around the plant.

This treatment is also good for young pines and gardenias that look pale green around the gills. It also works on baby pin oaks.

FRED'S SUPER TIP

One neat way to expand your indoor garden is to take slips or cuttings from new and different plants. Other gardeners are usually willing to offer you slips of their favorite plants.

It is best to root cuttings in a medium such as vermiculite, perlite or sphagnum peat moss. If you must use water,

be prepared to transplant as soon as
your cutting has roots that are 1/4 inch
long.

To get your slip or cutting, find a
piece of new growth on the parent
plant. Cut the stem just below a node
(where a leaf joins the stem). Strip
away any growth near the bottom of
the slip.

Rootone is a root stimulant that is
very beneficial when starting plants. It
is available at garden centers. Dip the
bottom of your cutting in Rootone
before placing it in your rooting medium. Whether you choose vermiculite,
perlite or sphagnum moss, the rooting
medium must stay damp throughout
the process.

Put your container and plant in a
clear plastic bag and tie the bag shut. If
your cutting is particularly tall, prop up
the bag with a popsicle stick. Open the
bag periodically to be sure the rooting
medium is damp. Do not place in direct
sunlight.

Tug gently on your cutting and as
soon as you feel resistance, it's ready to
be transplanted. It is a good idea to
transplant several slips into one pot.
They will grow best when the roots are
crowded. Put your potted cuttings in a
sunny spot. Transplant into separate
containers when the cuttings outgrow
their original pot.

Philodendron, dieffenbachia and rubber plants are all plants that are fairly
easy to slip.

October

✏️ October Checklist

LAWN TIPS

❑ Continue fertilizing your lawn every 4-6 weeks during fall and winter.
❑ Try any one of the many creative ways to rid your yard of moles.
❑ Aerate your lawn so it can breathe again.

EARLY

❑ Harvest green tomatoes before killing frost.
❑ Fall plow garden.
❑ Harvest sweet potatoes.
❑ Bring in all houseplants before temperatures drop below 55 degrees; check for insects and water less; do not repot.
❑ Keep weeds out of the garden
❑ Bring pots of gerbera daisies indoors.
❑ Plant a cover crop of rye or barley over the garden.
❑ Prepare Christmas cactuses for blooming.
❑ Plant trees.

MIDDLE

❑ Move those perennials.
❑ Harvest winter squash.
❑ Plant full-grown mums.
❑ Harvest horseradish roots.
❑ Wrap trunks of young, deciduous trees.
❑ Protect evergreens, azaleas and rhododendrons from drying winter winds.

LATE

❑ Plant spring-flowering bulbs to be forced indoors early next season.
❑ Prune trees.
❑ Clean and store tools, lawn mower and tiller.

SUPER TIP

❑ Planting the bulb garden.

ctober is for poets, fans of Indian summer and little children who want to parade around the neighborhood looking like ghosts, goblins and fairy princesses.

The leaves change into great bursts of crimson, russet and gold, the garden chores are almost finished, and it's time to sit on the back porch and reflect that another year has almost past — and it's so good to be a part of it.

October comes from the Latin word for "eight"; its location as the 10th month of the year is the work of the Romans. The average high temperature in the Louisville area is a crisp 69.2 degrees; the average low 46.2 degrees. The average October rainfall is 2.63 inches.

The wettest October in history was in 1883, when 8.05 inches fell. The driest October was in 1907, when only .07 inches of rain fell, the driest month in local history.

The highest recorded temperature for the month was 92 degrees, which occurred Oct. 2, 1953, and Oct. 4 and 5, 1959. The all-time low was 23 degrees, set on Oct. 29, 1925, and Oct. 23, 1952.

The earliest snowfall in local history occurred on Oct. 3, 1980, when a trace fell across Kentuckiana. The heaviest October snowfall was the 1.2 inches that fell on Oct. 23, 1937.

By the way, the average annual snowfall for the Louisville area is about 18 inches.

There are 11 hours and 48 minutes of sun on Oct. 1, and 10 hours and 37 minutes on Oct. 31. The average soil temperature varies from 53 to 62 degrees.

Columbus landed in America on Oct. 12, 1492, and slightly over 400 years later, on Oct. 1, 1896, free rural mail delivery began in the United States. The price has gone up considerably since.

LAWN TIPS

Not all of your yard problems are caused by tiny creatures that buzz, hum or burrow microscopic holes beneath your grass. Many of them come in larger packages, sometimes bark and even walk on two legs.

Then, of course, there is the question I've been asked exactly 4,267,952 times over the years: "Fred, what in the world can I do to get rid of my moles?"

Well, every problem, it seems, inspires a unique solution — or several unique solutions. Here are a few of the more interesting solutions I've received from gardeners over the years. Some of these animals are bigger pests in the garden than on the lawn, but they all run together in the urban landscape.

MOLES — Let's deal with this one with a little honesty: Unless you've got the time and patience to stalk moles as they feed — or are willing to place guillotine-like traps along their burrows — there's no one good way to rid your yard of these creatures.

And even traps aren't always 100 percent effective.

There is also one newer remedy

that uses a mix of castor oil and detergent, but we'll get to that after some mole history.

Moles are a very formidable foe. They have squishy, torpedo shaped bodies 5 to 6 inches long. They feed on earthworms, grubs, slugs and ants and have such a highly developed sense of touch in the tips of their noses they can "feel" an earthworm burrowing two feet away. They can burrow from 100 to 300 feet a day and will eat their own weight in food — about 5 grams — everyday.

Moles will eat some seeds, roots and vegetable matter, but most of the problems they cause come from the opportunistic mice who cruise their tunnels behind them.

Steel traps will help — over time. Find the burrow, set the trap over it and check it daily. I've also known people who simply pulled up a lawn chair when moles are most active — early in the morning and early in the evening — and watched the burrows for activity. A quick thrust with a pitchfork, or shovel, eliminated the pest. You can also use a pesticide in the fall to eliminate grubs from your lawn, but the earthworms, which you don't want to harm, will remain.

Some people have suggested placing chewing gum in the runs, the theory being that the moles eat it and gum themselves to death. Some say to dump bleach in the runs, that the odor will drive them out. Some companies sell little "vibrating windmills" that stick in the ground and are supposed to drive the sensitive little creatures away. If you want to risk the dangers to domestic animals — and even children — there are poison pellets you can buy to place in the mole runs.

Finally, I received a recipe for castor oil and detergent a couple of years ago that has worked for me.

Whip up 3 ounces of castor oil and 3 tablespoons of a liquid detergent in a blender. Then add 8 tablespoons of water and blend again until frothy.

Using a 15-gallon, hose-attached sprayer, put 15 tablespoons of mix into the sprayer jar. Fill the remainder of the jar with water. Walking at a slow pace, spray the solution on your lawn, then water it into your soil with a sprinkler.

Oh, yeah. Be sure to do this about 1 a.m. because then your next door neighbor won't know why he has all the moles and you don't — and you sure don't want them back.

Some people plant castor-oil plants around their yards, which also is supposed to help, but I'm very leery of that because the plant's beans are toxic.

By the way, the castor-oil-and-detergent-solution method was used by the Kentucky Fair & Exposition Center's grounds crew at the University of Louisville's practice football field. It seems Coach Howard Schnellenberger was steaming over moles tearing up his practice field.

RABBITS — Bugs Bunny may be an amusing cartoon character, but his real-life counterpart isn't very funny. The surest solution, of course, is to build a chicken-wire fence about 18 inches tall around the garden so rabbits can't get through. It's often only needed during the winter or early spring; rabbits aren't near the problem when other food is available.

Horticulturists at the University of Illinois found one way to keep rabbits away from the early spring beans and peas was to dust the vegetables with baby powder. It has to be baby powder, they said, not talcum powder.

DOGS — Much as you love your dog — or even your neighbor's dog — allowing them to use your lawn as a "rest stop" often leaves unsightly messes. Urine spots can cause round, dead spots in a lawn, and heavier matter is unsightly and dangerous to pedestrians. Injured spots in the lawn can often be repaired by soaking the spots with water and reseeding, if necessary.

RACCOONS AND GROUNDHOGS — Ermal Kellem of Corydon, Ind., told me about a solution to these critters that's always worked for him — especially when it comes to his corn. He puts 3 ounces of cayenne pepper in a half-gallon of water and slowly boils it for 20 minutes. When it cools, he sprays it on the corn.

SQUIRRELS — Kellem's "Cayenne Connection" might also work on tomato plants in order to control squirrels. Another gardener I know said he stops squirrels by putting a pan of dried dog food next to the tomatoes. He claims the squirrels would rather eat the dog chow than his Better Boys.

Another method is to lay down chicken wire, neatly cutting and fitting the wire around the plants. This is like a "cattle guard" approach — the squirrels don't like to walk on the mesh, apparently for fear of getting their toes caught.

CHIPMUNKS — These little critters are also very cute, but they cause serious structural problems as they burrow under walls, pools and foundations. They also can hurt the look of your carefully planned lawn by eating spring bulbs such as daffodils or tulips.

To avoid that, place your bulbs inside wire cages made of hardware cloth. Both squirrels and chipmunks can be caught in "live traps." Peanut butter is a great bait, but be sure to leave the trap "unset" for a week so the animal can get accustomed to eating in such a wiry environment.

After you catch them, be sure to take them at least 10 miles outside the city limits. Any less than that, and they will beat you back home.

BIRDS — Although birds on the lawn are often fun to watch — and listen to — large numbers of them may be delivering a message; they may be feeding on the grubs that could be eating the heck out of your grass roots. So regard them as a possible indicator of trouble.

In the garden, large birds such as crows and grackles sometimes pull up seedlings or chop them in half. One solution is to stretch a nylon cord from one end of the row to the other directly above the row — and about 2 inches high. Remove the cord when the plants are about 6 inches high.

MOSQUITOES — Ah, the music of

summer: Slap. Slap. Slap.

But here I want to warn you about something that doesn't work. Every spring I see ads in the paper for the "citrosa plant," which is supposedly guaranteed to repel mosquitoes. Most of these plants are nothing more than scented geraniums and don't work as mosquitoe chasers, especially since the only way to release their "perfume" is to crush their leaves.

Purple martins, if you can lure them, will eat thousands of mosquitoes. But nothing works better than a screened porch.

DEER — The best — and most expensive — solution is a sturdy fence about 8 to 10 feet high. Another is to hang bars of Dial soap around the perimeter of the yard; its odor offends deer. But be sure to hang the bars at the branch tips; rabbits like the soap taste and will come hopping if the soap runs down the trunk in the rain.

Another solution is an organic fertilizer called Miloganite, which is made — I promise — from Milwaukee sewage sludge. Deer don't like its smell.

PEOPLE CREATURES — We continually walk on the ground or drive cars and trucks across it to carry trees and shrubs to their appointed places, all of which seriously compacts the soil. That's a problem that can be cured with an "aerator," a medieval-looking device that will drive little spike holes in your lawn allowing it to breath again. You can rent them, or rent a professional to do it.

You do want your lawn to be able to say, "Ahhhhhhh," don't you?

GARDEN TIPS
EARLY

We're starting to get near the time when frost will zap your tomato plants. If the weatherman calls for a frost, you can save a lot of those green tomatoes by picking them and bringing them indoors to ripen.

The easiest way is to pull up several whole vines and hang them in a dry storage area or shed. I wouldn't bring them indoors to the basement because many tomatoes are infected with whiteflies this time of year.

I prefer to pick tomatoes that are mature and green or just beginning to change color. We use the smaller ones for pickling.

Keep the ripest tomatoes at room temperature, and they should ripen in a week. Mature green tomatoes should be spread out in a single layer OUT OF DIRECT LIGHT. At 60 to 70 degrees they'll ripen in two weeks. Wrapping each tomato in old newspaper or the pages of an old phone book keeps them in good condition.

Another way to ripen tomatoes indoors came from a friend who is not an expert in gardening but in sports— Cawood Ledford. He said he had good luck putting green tomatoes in a Styrofoam cooler along with an apple or two. The apples give off ethylene gas, which promotes ripening.

If you can, try plowing the garden now to get it ready for next year. It will get you off to a quicker start next spring, will allow the ground to warm up faster and will help the compost or leaves you add to the soil rot more efficiently.

It's about time to harvest your sweet potatoes. They are best harvested when the vines begin to yellow. Even a light frost will kill the vines, and soil temperatures below 50 degrees will damage the tuber.

After digging the potatoes, leave them exposed for two to three hours to dry thoroughly, then move them to a warm, humid room or area for two weeks to totally cure.

These conditions are hard to produce, but I had good luck storing them in a black plastic bag in front of a sunny window in the attic of the garage and even in the basement. Sweet potatoes actually improve during storage because part of their starch content turns to sugar.

Every October I get calls from people about houseplants loosing their leaves after they've been brought back  indoors for the winter. In every case the gardener waited too long to bring the plant inside, although a change in the amount of light a plant gets will also cause some leaf drop.

In any event, bring them in before nighttime temperatures drop to 55 degrees.

And don't bring the insects indoors with the plants. If the plant is small, tie a plastic bag around the pot and stem and wash the leaves in soapy water.

For larger plants use a garden hose, or insecticide, being sure to get under the leaves.

You don't want to repot the indoor plants that have been outside all summer, even if they have long roots coming out of their drainage holes. Repotting will only encourage growth at a time when the plants need to take a break. Just take a sharp knife and cut off the roots. And remember, don't use fertilizer during the fall and winter. That also encourages growth.

Water less—only when the top inch of soil feels dry or if the foliage begins to droop. Never let the plants sit in water. It encourages root rot.

As hard as it can be to maintain your gardening enthusiasm this time of year, it's important to keep your garden as weed-free as possible. Many of the most noxious weeds go to seed this time of year, and if you deal with them now, you won't have to deal with their children and grandchildren next year.

If you're totally desperate and behind in your chores, run the lawn mower over the garden plot to keep the weeds from forming seed heads, and then till the ground.

Big, proud gerbera daisies have become very popular in recent years, but they will not survive outdoors all winter. Since the daisies are traditionally raised in pots, just bring the pots indoors and keep them near bright sun; also, keep the soil moist and warm. Otherwise they may go dormant and die back to the soil. You want to keep them rested but not comatose. Next spring just plant the whole pot in the ground. They're easier to care for that way.

Here's a reminder: A cover crop of rye or barley sown over the garden can be very beneficial if you haven't been able to plow this fall. When it is plowed under next spring it will add organic matter to the soil and will protect the ground from erosion all winter. The seeds for such crops can be broadcast by hand.

Another reminder that if you want your Thanksgiving and Christmas cactuses to bloom for the holidays, they need bright sun during the day and COMPLETE darkness at night. Light, even from a street light, will throw the plants off schedule. It's also important to withhold water from the cactuses. Don't let  them get bone-dry, but keep them on the dry side.

Once the buds have formed, gradually resume normal watering and bring them into a bright room where you can enjoy them all day.

October—and even November— is also an excellent time to plant trees. Most woody plants need less water in the fall to survive, and even if a tree is without leaves its roots will continue to grow as long as the soil is moist and the ground temperature is above 40 degrees. The roots can get a better, ah, foot hold, without competition from the leaves. Then, in the spring, the leaves can take advantage of a strong root system. It's one big, happy partnership.

For the most part I am very much opposed to fast-growing trees. They are often weak-limbed, have invasive roots and cause more problems than they are worth. But there are some "compromise" trees that will work well in the landscape, mixing faster growth with other benefits.

Here's a list of those trees you should consider:

Bald cypress— A deciduous conifer best known for its swamp growth, the bald cypress will also do well in the home landscape. Give it lots of room.

Japanese zelkova — A vase-shaped tree with great fall color, often touted as a replacement for the much-lamented American elm.

Red maple — A faster-growing tree that's showy in the spring when it buds out and in the fall when the leaves turn red, yellow and scarlet. Look for "Red Sunset" or "October Glory" varieties.

River birch — A fast grower that's not as prone to the birch borer. Looks great on a front lawn, but give it room to spread.

Tulip poplar — A little weak-limbed, but quick-growing. It produces light to moderate shade.

Lace bark elm — A beautiful tree that only gets better with age as bark "peels" away from trunk in delicate whorls.

Red oak — Among the fastest-growing of the oaks with good fall color.

Willow oak — An interesting tree with the leaves of a willow tree but the body of an oak tree. It's rounded and provides moderate shade.

One of the more popular plants to, uh, "pop up" in the last few years have been ornamental grasses. Their colors — from an airy green to burning red — are amazing, as are their many shapes and sizes. Some are a foot tall while others can soar to 12 feet.

Beyond that, by the time October arrives, many will toss up billowy plumes that are just gorgeous in a fall setting, especially with a setting sun behind them. Most ornamental grasses are also very tough, and most insects leave them alone, making them even more of a treat. The only care they take is giving them a "hair cut" in late winter. Cut them to within 2 or 3 inches of the ground in early March.

Some nurseries specialize in ornamental grasses. A few of the more popular varieties are Japanese blood grass, maiden grass (miscanthus sineses gracillimus) and Oriental fountain grass (pennisetum orientale).

To really appreciate their beauty and variety, you must see them yourself, either pictured in a catalog, or better yet, in person. Once you do, your landscape will never be the same.

MIDDLE

Cruise around all parts of your perennial garden and look for lilies, irises, peonies and others that can be moved while there is still some sunshine. It's getting very late. They can be moved now if you must, but this should have been done in July.

If you've been waiting to harvest your winter squash, the ol' calendar on the wall says it's time to get moving. Acorn, spaghetti and butternut squash are ready when the fruit turns a deeper, solid color and the rind is hard.

Butternut squash will turn from greenish-yellow to solid tan, spaghetti squash changes from light to bright yellow, and acorn squash adds a bronze or orange glow on a dark-green back ground. Leave a two-inch hunk of the stem on the squash to protect the fruit from rot.

If you're tired of a dull, dreary flower garden, a garden that was done in by hot, dry weather, you can brighten the scene considerable by planting full-grown mums now.

Mums — or chrysanthemums for long — are one flower you can transplant when in full bloom. They should be planted before hard winter weather to give them a chance to get established. The U.S. Department of Agriculture suggests you prepare a soil bed about

10 days before you plant. Dig and loosen the soil to a depth of six inches. Just before planting, respade the soil bed to kill weeds seeds that have germinated.

As you plant the mums — and there are dozens of colors and varieties, so plan carefully — press the soil firmly to eliminate air pockets. Space them from two to 2 1 /2 feet apart in well-drained soil. Water well, and you could have color into November.

After the hard frost does hit, cut the tops to ground level and mulch, which will protect them against winter freezing and thawing. When they begin growing again next year, pinch them back several times to force them to spread.

If you're growing horseradish — the perfect Derby Day condiment — remember that it makes its greatest growth in late summer and autumn. For that reason, harvesting the roots is best done just before the ground freezes.

Remember to cut off "sets" of roots eight to 14 inches long to refrigerate over the winter. In the spring you can begin next season's crop.

Here's another reminder to wrap all your young, deciduous trees with long strips of burlap or sisal paper to pre- · vent sunscald and frost damage. Such damage occurs during warm days and freezing nights. This weakens the tree, and a severe winter or dry spell the next summer can kill it.

Evergreens, including azaleas and rhododendrons, are very susceptible to drying winter winds. If you have a small clump, you can protect it behind a burlap screen—burlap stapled to four stakes driven into the ground. Or you can buy a can of antidesiccant spray. The spray coats the plant with latex, allowing it to breathe but not lose moisture. Use it just before serious cold weather sets in.

LATE

It's not too late to plant some bulbs in pots so you can force them to bloom indoors early next spring. Place choice bulbs in a pot with their tips above the soil, moisten the soil and refrigerate for 10 to 13 weeks. Then move to a cool, bright room and water.

Fall and early winter are good times to prune your trees. It is a very tricky process that must be done correctly or you can seriously damage the tree.

If you're just doing some trimming, be sure your pruning cuts are made flush with the tree. If you leave stubs, they may rot, which could damage the trunk and inner tissue.

In general, you should remove dead limbs, limbs that rub together and narrow, V-shaped crotches.

If you're putting away your tools for the winter, clean off all the mud. Wipe the blades of the clippers and pruners and apply a few drops of oil to all moving parts. Dig out all the booklets and warranty information that came with your mower and tiller to find out how to properly store them for the winter.

FRED'S TIPS

Any nuts that happen to be growing on trees around your house should be allowed to mature fully on the tree and then fall naturally, or with some mild shaking. Gather them daily and allow them to air-dry. Store them in a cool, dry area.

Heavy rains often bring a crop of mushrooms popping up through the ground, usually in places where old lumber, logs or tree roots are buried. They will not damage the lawn and will disappear in colder, drier weather. If you can't wait, just mow them down or rake them up.

If you're planting ground cover in the fall, be sure to put down a two-inch layer of mulch to protect the baby plants. Otherwise freezing and thawing can heave them out of the ground.

If you're thinking of planting some trees this fall, you're better off avoiding magnolia, dogwood, sweet gum and yellowwood. They are unusually susceptible to winter damage and are better planted in the spring.

If trees and shrubs are newly planted, you should withhold fertilizer for a year to allow the plant to get well-established in its new home. Then you can give it a growing boost.

Octobers go much easier if you have a handy stack of cloth, plastic sheets, newspapers, cardboard boxes, wooden boxes or old drapes to serve as protection against frost. Often there will be a hard freeze followed by several more weeks of warm Indian summer, and if you protect your flowers, you can keep the colors alive for a long time.

As tough as it can be to do, now is a good time to take a good look at the trees in your yard to determine if they are growing too close together. We all hate to remove trees, especially those we've nursed from babies, but if you weed them out, the survivors will be stronger, healthier and will probably fill in the gap left by the missing tree. So be fair, but be firm. You're better off in the long run.

Here's a tip that could raise a stink even if it works. Henry Converse, a member of the Kentucky Nut Growers Association, reported that squirrels can be repelled by emptying the contents of cat-litter boxes around the bases of nut trees. The litter can even be placed in perforated bags and hung from the trees, but it must be replaced as the odor fades or dries out. If you have a lot of nut trees, however, you'll need a lot of cats.

Onions can be easily stored by braiding the tops together and hanging them in the kitchen for easy access. They may create a "tearful" odor for a time, but the onions will also be very handy.

If you're looking way down the road and want to plant trees that will produce a wide variety of fall colors, here are a few trees and their autumn colors: red maple, intense red; sugar maple, orange and yellow; sumac, deep scarlet; black gum and ash, deep wine; red oak, dull red; white oak, hazy brown; hickory, light gold; elm, lemon.

If you want to avoid bringing a lot of bugs into your house along with the firewood, you can minimize the problem by taking a few precautions. Don't stack the wood against the house or another building; it keeps the bugs dry and warm. Bring in only the wood you can burn in a few days. Do not leave firewood in the house over the summer. Don't bother with insecticides; it's unnecessary and expensive and could be hazardous to your health when you burn the wood.

All those leaves falling from your trees can greatly improve your garden soil, especially heavy clay and sandy soils. If possible — and just running over them with the lawn mower will help — shred the leaves before spreading them over the garden. Then till them in. You'll be amazed at how your soil will improve in a few years.

FRED'S SUPER TIP

Home gardeners are coming out of nurseries these days with armloads of bags filled with bulbs. Mention bulbs and most people think of tulips, hyacinths and narcissus. But the truth is flowering bulbs come in an almost unending array and produce blooms of various sizes and colors.

With careful planning, your spring bulb garden can have bright splashes of color beginning with the yellow winter aconite in February or March and lasting through the final late-blooming tulip in May.

Planning on paper is an easy way to redecorate your garden. Bulbs require little garden space and can be planted in annual and perennial flower beds, among shrubs, under trees and in almost every part of the landscape.

Begin your bulb plan by making a scale drawing of your garden area. Roughly draw in where you would like bulbs to be planted. Check the growing conditions of the area. Remember, the most important element in growing bulbs in our clay-type soil is GOOD DRAINAGE. Dig a hole about six inches deep and fill it with water. If the water is still there an hour later, choose another location. When planting, check the depth chart that comes with the package. A general rule of thumb is to plant the bulb about three times deeper than its own length, and, please, please, pointed side up.

If the soil is very hard and dry, use an auger the diameter of your bulbs. Attach it to your electric drill, and wrap a piece of white tape around the auger at the depth you want to plant the bulb. It's a heckuva lot faster and easier on the wrist than using a hand-planter.

Plant snowdrops, anemone and crocus for borders, grape hyacinth, oxalis and scilla for four to eight-inch tall blooms and tulips, narcissus and hyacinths as background plantings.

Spring-flowering bulbs should be planted in October to insure good root development before winter. The better the root system, the better the flowers will be in the spring. Buy early and be sure to select large, firm, plump bulbs or roots. Do not purchase any that are bruised, blemished or soft.

If you do not get a chance to plant them in October, don't fret. I have planted tulips as late as January. That was not by choice, however, I forgot where I put them in the storage shed.

As further proof that late fall planting works, have you ever enjoyed the tulip gardens at Churchill Downs during Derby Week? Donnie Lord, the Downs chief gardener, does all of his spring tulip planting after the fall racing meet is over and that is usually after Thanksgiving.

If you don't get them in the ground, toss them out. They will never survive a full year out of the ground.

When you dig the hole for the spring bulbs, put a little bone meal in the bottom of the hole for good root development. But remember, the most important time to feed bulbs is in the spring, just as the new growth is beginning to develop from the ground.

Are you a patio gardener? You can enjoy tulips next spring if you plant bulbs this fall in boxes or other containers that are at least a foot deep and have drainage holes. I know one gardener who has had spring bulbs in planters around his condominium every year for the last six years, regardless of how cold the winters get.

November

✎ November Checklist

LAWN TIPS

❑ Mow grass to a height of about 1 1/2 to 2 inches for the winter.
❑ Rake every last leaf off of your lawn before winter comes.

EARLY

❑ Remove leaves and any weak stems from bottoms of roses.
❑ Plant deciduous trees; stake for support.
❑ Sketch out what you'd like to plant next year; clean up the garden; fall plow.
❑ Consider building a compost heap.
❑ Move houseplants closer to sunny windows; water less frequently and withhold fertilizer.
❑ Force bulbs indoors for spring blooming.
❑ Continue preparing poinsettias to put out red bracts.
❑ Put screens around smaller trees to keep rabbits and mice away.
❑ Dig the hole for living Christmas tree.
❑ Complete harvest and storage of root crops.
❑ Collect seeds from flowers and store.
❑ Transplant scented geraniums, creeping rosemary, lemon verbena and bay and move indoors.

MIDDLE

❑ Continue to water evergreens; tie up branches to avoid damage from heavy accumulations of ice and snow.
❑ Drain and cover bird baths; stock bird feeders.
❑ Stock up on gardening materials for next season.
❑ Continue to plant hardy bulbs; take in tubers and corms from dahlias, caladiums, cannas and gladioluses.
❑ Cut mums back to ground level.
❑ Fertilize trees after first killing frost.
❑ Finish harvesting gourds.

LATE

❑ Cut roses back, spray with miticide and fungicide and mulch.
❑ Mulch strawberry plants.
❑ Remove any remaining fruit from fruit trees and clean area underneath to discourage rodents.

SUPER TIP

❑ Safely burning firewood.

Ah, November, with its cheerful fires, Thanksgiving celebrations and, if you're lucky, time for just one more walk in the woods before the snow flies.

November is the month when the bright colors give way to yellows and grays, and winter's frozen breath creeps under the doors and past windows. But it's also the height of football season, and can basketball be far behind?

November takes its name from *novem*, the Latin word for nine. Because July was named for Julius Caesar and August for Augustus Caesar, the Roman senate did offer to name November after Tiberius Caesar. He declined, saying, "What would you do if there are 13 emperors?"

The average high temperature in November is 55.5 degrees; the average low 36.6 degrees. The average precipitation — melted snow included — is 3.49 inches.

The most precipitation ever in November is the 9.12 inches that fell in 1957; the least was the .25 inches in 1904. The highest recorded temperature in November was 84 degrees on Nov. 17, 1958. The coldest day was minus 1 degree on Nov. 25, 1950.

The average first date for snowfall in our area is Nov. 16, although it can fall well before — or after — that. The normal snowfall for the month is 1.5 inches, but 13.2 inches fell in November 1966, including 13 inches on one day, Nov. 3, in Louisville. The odd

thing was the temperature never dropped below 34 degrees, and the snow was extremely heavy and wet, killing thousands of birds at a nearby poultry farm.

There are 10 hours and 35 minutes of sun on Nov. 1 and nine hours and 45 minutes on Nov. 30. The average soil temperature ranges between 50 and 54 degrees.

The first intercollegiate football game in the United States was played on Nov. 6, 1869, between Rutgers and Princeton, and Saturday and Sunday meals in this country have been eaten in front of television sets ever since.

LAWN TIPS

Oh, boy. It's finally November, the lawn is asleep and you won't need the lawn mower again until late March or April.

That's true — if you've cut your grass to about 1 1/2 to 2 inches to get it ready for winter. Otherwise, pick a warm day and mow it one more time.

And here — once again courtesy of the University of Kentucky — are the specific reasons why grass needs a very short haircut heading into winter.

There will be a pop quiz on this at the end of the section, so follow carefully.

Basically, your lawn is always changing and regenerating itself — much more than you ever realized. The basic unit of grass is called a "tiller." Each tiller grows 3 or 4 functional leaves — the things you cut off by the millions every summer. Each leaf lives only three to four weeks. Each tiller lives from a few weeks to about 18 months.

New tillers are produced from buds in the bases (axils) of the leaves in a fashion very similar to branches of a tree. Depending on the type of grass, these buds form as underground rhizomes or above-ground stolons. Either way they are connected for a short time to their parent tiller. But by the time you see the leaves of grass, they may be fully independent.

A tiller will produce a new leaf every few days, stopping when temperatures consistently fall below 40 degrees. Growth resumes when the weather warms in the spring.

So far so good, right?

Then listen carefully to this:

In the fall the temperature drops, and the autumn rains replenish soil water, promoting tiller growth. As the season turns cooler the top growth slows, but root growth continues in the warmer soil. The newer plant cells are smaller, but have thicker walls and smaller cell cavities. Sugars and proteins accumulate in the cells, acting as an antifreeze, helping to prevent freezing.

While all this growth is occurring, the hours of sunlight are diminishing. Your turf can't support all this activity. Either the number of tillers must be reduced — or the tiller size must be reduced.

Enter your lawn mower. You cut off the leaves, and more tillers survive, getting your turf ready for the next year. Fall fertilization — as you've seen in previous months — also improves the production, growth and survival of these tillers.

Close-mowing also removes the frost-tender cells; the hardier cells continue to grow, but at a much slower pace. That's important because in Kentucky cool-season grasses such as bluegrass will grow even in mid-January if sunlight hits the green tissue and temperatures exceed 40 degrees.

If you let your grass grow into winter too tall — say 5 inches — the weaker, unhealthy tillers will die or "brown out," weakening and thinning your lawn.

Another reason for close-mowing — and fall fertilization — is that in the spring many tillers do their reproductive thing, "go to seed," and then die. If you don't have a new and healthy crop of "non-flowering" tillers coming behind the dead tillers, the grass will also become very thin as the old ones die out. Fertilizing in the spring only aggravates this condition as it promotes new top growth at the expense of a good, solid root system.

And I was only kidding about the pop quiz.

Leaf removal — repeat 100 times after me: Never leave old leaves on the lawn. Never leave old leaves on the lawn. Never leave old leaves on the lawn. . . .

If you do leave old leaves on the lawn, they will mat, smother the grass, weaken it and prevent it from getting through the winter.

Raking leaves is one of the rites of fall.

Don't be wrong about it.

GARDEN TIPS
EARLY

Just because it's early November doesn't mean it's time to send roses "beddy-bye" for the year. Don't get in a big hurry to cut them back and winterize them. Most rose growers I know like to have two or three nights when temperatures drop into the low 20s before they begin the process.

You need several cold nights to harden the stems and slow down the upward movement of water. That should occur in a few weeks.

Is there anything you can do in the meantime? Sure. Put on a pair of gloves and strip off the leaves to about 15 inches above ground. Then take a good look at the plant. If you see any small, weak, spindly stems, remove them. Leave five good, strong stems on each plant.

Most years, early November remains a good time to plant deciduous plants because even if their tops are dormant, the root system can continue to grow and become well-established. However, I would plant only balled and burlapped or container-grown plants; bare-root planting is very tricky this time of year.

In checking trees for purchase, be sure the branch tips have healthy buds with just a little sign of green. Check the ends of some branches by lightly nicking them with your fingernail. A live branch will show a little green. Please be careful; if 100 people check the same tree it could be killed by "Fingernail Fungus."

Large trees should be supported with stakes driven into the soil outside the planting hole. One trick is to save your old garden hose, then cut it into small sections and thread the support string through it.

Bend the hose around the tree; this will keep the string from cutting into the bark. Wrap the trees in special tree wrap to protect them from the freeze-thaw cycle.

November is a good time to look over the past growing season and plan next year's activities. Draw a sketch of what you have and what you plan to add. Makes notes on what worked and what didn't; there's room at the back of every chapter in this book to do just that.

Give your planning some thought. Look ahead a few years. A tiny tree planted now could be eating your eaves in 10 years. The gardening pace has slowed now and you have time to think and to scan the catalogs.

Don't forget to clean up your garden, fall-plow it if possible and have your soil tested to see what nutrients you'll need for next year. It's so important you do that.

Think about starting a compost bin so you can improve your soil later this fall or early next spring.

It's easy. One simple way is to just pound four stakes in the ground for corners, and wrap hardware cloth about three feet tall around them. Build your compost pile near the garden. Dump in shredded leaves and grass clippings until they are about six to 10 inches deep. Then sprinkle on 1 1/2 cups of 10-10-10 fertilizer and 2/3 cup of dolomitic limestone. Keep adding layers of leaves, clippings, garbage scraps and fertilizer. You'll be amazed at how quickly the compost will "work" if you keep the pile moist and keep turning it over with a rake or shovel. It will make the perfect garden additive.

As houseplant growth slows, apply less and less fertilizer and water. You might move the plants closer to sunnier windows if they are dropping too many leaves, although that's normal for many plants this time of year.

It's not too late to "force" bulbs indoors for early spring. Pot a few with the tips of the bulbs just above the soil line, moisten the soil and refrigerate for 10 to 13 weeks. Then transfer to a cool, sunny location and allow three to four weeks for the indoor blooms.

Continue keeping your poinsettias in complete darkness for 14 to 15 hours. But please, please remember to put them in bright light the rest of the time. I can't tell you how many times people have left their plants in the closet 24 hours a day, then wondered why they died.

Continue the process until the red bracts begin to show, then put them in cool, bright light. If you keep them in a cool room, they'll bloom for weeks after Christmas.

Tour the yard. Be sure to place metal screens around the smaller trees to keep the rabbits and mice from gnawing at the bark. Sometimes you can buy enough old screens at a yard sale to provide tree protection for years. Hardware cloth works well too.

Keep the screen a few inches away from the trunk and push it a few inches into the ground to keep the burrowing rodents away. A short rod or stick will help. If you don't use screening, at least pull all the mulch a few inches away from the tree so the rodents won't spend the winter living next to it.

If you're planning to order a live Christmas tree, it will help to dig the hole now while the digging is good. Put the dirt in buckets or baskets and store it in the garage or basement.

Finish harvesting your root crops and store them in a cool, humid location. If humidity is a problem, store them in perforated plastic bags, which will help.

If you feel adventurous, you might try collecting seeds from some of your favorite flowers and storing them in small, airtight containers at a temperature of 35 to 55 degrees.

Be warned: If you collect hybrid seeds, the flowers you grow next year may not be exactly the same as those you planted; hybrid seeds will revert to one of their ancestors.

That may not matter. I know of marigolds that came up "volunteer" year after year in the same spot with no appreciable change in color or tenacity. It's always fun to keep a little of last summer for next summer.

Scented geraniums, creeping rosemary, lemon verbena and bay are not hardy in this area, so transplant them into pots so they can be moved indoors, or into a cold frame.

Another shrub that's rapidly growing in popularity in this area is the deciduous holly, a holly plant that loses its leaves in the winter while it holds onto its bright red, orange or yellow berries, giving it a beauty all its own.

You'll need at least one male of the species for each eight to 10 females to insure pollination — and good berries. The plants will grow from 3 to 15 feet tall, and some may even be pruned as trees, which make a wonderful conversation piece in the winter garden.

There's not much special about these plants in the summer — perhaps a show of tiny white flowers. When situated against the right background — perhaps a white or gray wall — the berries make a stunning winter display, at least until the birds discover them. Some of the more popular varieties are sparkleberry, winter red and cacapon, but there are many others, often labeled under the generic name "winterberry." Check them out for your winter garden.

MIDDLE

Soak all the soil around your newer plantings, especially evergreens, to help them through the winter. Use an anti-desiccant spray on especially vulnerable rhododendrons and azaleas. You can even tie up the branches of pyramidal arborvitae and other upright evergreens with heavy twine to avoid possible damage from heavy ice and snow accumulations, although such storms do not occur in this area every winter.

Drain and cover bird baths and shallow garden pools to avoid winter damage and get to work buying or repairing the bird feeders — the birds will need some winter feed soon enough. Your local Audubon Society chapter often sponsors autumn bird-seed sales, with the profits going to help the organization, so watch for a sale.

If you do a lot of outdoor gardening — or indoor for that matter — this is the season to stock up on planting soil, fertilizer, pre-emergents, mulch and peat moss at bargain rates. Be sure to check bags for damage and spills.

You can continue to plant tulips, daffodils, crocus, lilies and other hardy bulbs as long as you can work the ground, or at least until Thanksgiving. Well-drained soil is essential for good bulbs. Most prefer partial shade. Mass them in large groupings for better effect.

If you haven't taken in the dahlia, caladium, canna and gladiolus tubers for winter storage, you're asking for trouble. All are vulnerable to heavy frost. Store them in a cool, dry place. Check monthly and throw out the rotten ones.

Cut mums back to ground level after they are finished blooming and cover with a light mulch after the first hard freeze.

Fertilize your trees with a high-nitrogen fertilizer AFTER the first hard killing frost; applying fertilizer too soon will promote growth that could be killed by the winter cold. The general recommendation is three pounds of actual nitrogen per 1,000 square feet of root area. Fertilize at least twice the distance from the trunk to the drip line to ensure that all feeder roots get some nourishment.

Finish harvesting your gourds. Wash them well, let them dry for four weeks and protect them with wax or even clear shellac.

LATE

OK, it should be about time to put those roses to bed for the winter. The late Charlie Dawson, a good friend and one of Kentucky's foremost rose growers, always recommended a final spraying of miticide to kill red spider mites as part of the final chores.

So cut the roses back to about 12 to 14 inches, remove any remaining foliage, spray them with a mix of miticide and fungicide. You should never mix anything with a miticide during the growing season, but in the dormant season it's fine.

You can mulch with any good shredded or chunk bark mulch, or you can use garden dirt. Be sure the soil is from another part of the garden so you don't dig around the roses and injure the roots .

If you are prepared and brought in some soil last month to stash between the roses, you can get a jump on the project. Plus you'll have some mulch material handy in the event of a cold snap.

Whatever material you use, mound it over the base of the plant at least eight to 10 inches high. It will settle, and you may have to add more mulch later. In a really cold winter, you might heap it over the stubs.

Be sure not to mulch too early. Wait until the ground has a crust to it. The mulch isn't to keep the plants warm over the winter. It's to keep the ground at a fairly cold temperature so the plants don't heave out in the winter months.

Climbing roses also need protection when winter temperatures drop near zero. When such weather is near, lay the canes on the ground, hold them down with pins or notched stakes and cover them with several inches of mulch stored in the garage.

If you have tree roses, wrap the heads of the plants in straw and cover with burlap. If sub-zero weather is on the way, dig carefully under the roots on one side of the plants — it may take a jackhammer — and pull the plants over, being careful not to break the root connectors. Then cover them with soil and straw. Come spring, set the plants upright again. It makes it easier for the Japanese beetles to find them.

It's also time to prepare your strawberries for a long winter's nap. Strawberries have shallow root systems, which are very susceptible to breaking when the ground freezes. Plan to apply a mulch to strawberries after growth has slowed, often following a week of temperatures in the 40s in the day and in the 20s at night but before the thermometer hits the single-digit numbers.

You should mulch strawberries with clean wheat straw. One year while mulching our strawberries, I ran out of straw, got too lazy to go to town for more and used some old, broken hay bales a neighbor offered me. I lived to regret it. The next year I had more weeds than strawberries and ended up plowing under the whole row.

Use about a bale of straw for each 50 feet of strawberry row and fluff it about three inches deep. Next spring, remove the mulch before the berries set out buds so you don't break off the crowns while removing it. Pile the straw between rows because it might be needed again in a cold snap.

You can also help your young fruit trees through the winter by harvesting any fruit that remains and cleaning an area of grass about two feet around the trunk to discourage rodents. Some orchard growers I know also put pea-size gravel around the trunk about 4 to 6 inches wide and deep. It discourages rodents and gives the trees more stability over the winter. Don't do any pruning of grapes or fruit trees now. Wait until the end of February or the first of March.

FRED'S TIPS

While tramping through the woods this fall, you're likely to see a small tree that might look good in your yard. Some of these trees can be moved — AFTER you get permission — but there are tricks to it.

First, be prepared to make two trips to the woods over a two-year period; the first trip to prune the roots, the second to come back a year later and do the moving.

To prune the roots, measure the diameter of the trunk, move out from it one foot for each inch of diameter, then dig a circular trench as deep as your spade can penetrate.

Refill the trench with topsoil, and the tree will form a dense mat of fibrous roots in that new dirt.

The second year — and be sure to move it in early spring or after a hard frost in the fall — you can dig up the tree and take it home. Water well and keep watering.

Very small trees can be moved immediately after a hard frost without digging a trench, but a tree of any size should be moved over a two-year period.

Be careful about changing a tree's habitat. It a tree has been living in the deep shade of the woods, it might die in an open spot in your lawn. It will, at the very least, take years to get going.

Houseplants often suffer from dry indoor air during the winter months, wilting and turning brown at the edges. You can help by humidifying the air around them or placing a tray of wet pebbles below them. Be sure the water in the pebble tray is well below the pot so it doesn't "wick" up into the pot.

Plants grown in containers are less cold-hardy than those grown in the garden because their roots are more exposed to freezing temperatures. You can insulate the roots by burying the pots in the ground or under a pile of sawdust, compost or mulch.

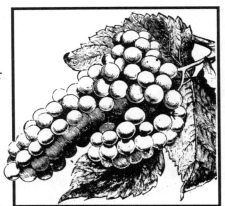

Many people will hastily put their spring bulbs in the ground in the fall, then forget where they put them. Make a chart of what you planted and where. More important, mark the locations with plastic sticks available at all gardening centers. Be sure to use an indelible pen listing the color and height of the plant and the date you put the bulb in the ground. It will prevent your bulbs from becoming lost children next spring.

Wild grape vines are best killed by cutting them off at ground level in late fall and applying an herbicide like Kleenup or Roundup to the green foliage in the spring. A repeat application might be needed later. Be careful not to get the chemical on other plants because it will kill them too.

To help protect your garden tools for next year, sharpen your spades, hoes,

shovels and lawn tools and cover them with a light coat of oil. Then they'll be ready to go in the spring.

If you're not sure how to dispose of your empty pesticide containers, the Division of Waste Management of the Kentucky Department for Environmental Protection recommends that you rinse the container three times, drain the rinse water into your sprayer tank for use, then wrap the container in a newspaper and put in the garbage. Plastic and metal containers should be punctured to be sure they are not used again.

We've talked a lot about mulching, but there's also a danger of over-mulching and suffocating the roots over a three- to five-year period. Outside of your roses, keep mulch only a few inches deep around your plants. That will be enough.

Root crops such as carrots, turnips and parsnips can be stored right where they grew in the garden. Cover them with a layer of straw, mulch, leaves or sawdust. It also makes them easier to dig in the winter.

Beets, cabbage, cauliflower, kale, leeks and onions can be stored for several weeks under mulch, but they probably won't last through the winter.

You can also bury a 20-gallon trash

container up to its lid in the garden, then pile straw or leaves over the top. It makes a nice root cellar for crop storage. Metal containers are more rodent-proof.

Spinach, although not a root crop, is so tough you can bury it under five inches of straw and harvest it all winter. In March, remove the straw and side-dress with ammonium nitrate, and the plants will put out new leaves way ahead of everyone else's.

Herbs such as thyme, parsley, dill, chives, mint and oregano can be grown indoors over the winter in a sunny window. Artificial light will work if you don't have a handy window. Pot some up and try it. Thyme, parsley and dill can be started from seed. You'll need cuttings for the others.

You can move your "magic lilies" any time after they have finished blooming and the flowers have faded. But don't put them in too much shade, which will inhibit their growth. It may take them a year or two after transplanting to fully bloom again.

Because most trees having a ropelike mesh of roots crisscrossing one another, you are often fertilizing many different trees when fertilizing the lawn. That's because most feeder roots grow within an inch of the surface. Keep that in mind when fertilizing and when contemplating construction projects. You never want to put a thick layer of new dirt beneath a healthy tree; it could kill it.

The old method of boring holes to fertilize trees isn't necessary. Granular or liquid fertilizer spread over the surface will do the trick.

Remember never to "top" your tree while pruning it. A lot of allegedly professional tree people will recommend it, but such topping throws off the balance between roots and tops, starving the root system. Topping also stimulates "rank" growth, which is soft and weak and opens the tree to disease.

If you bring a shrub or small tree home from the nursery and notice that it's pot-bound — the roots are massed and circling thickly around the inside of the pot or hanging out the bottom — there's still a way to plant it.

Take the shrub out of its container, use a sharp spade or shovel to cut through the rootball from 1/3 to 1/2 way up from the bottom, and then literally pull the remaining roots apart, forming an opening.

When planting, press the rootball into the bottom of the hole, fill around the roots and water. Trimming the roots and opening the bottom will encourage the growth of pot-bound plants.

Buying the biggest tree in the nursery isn't always the best idea. Small and medium-sized trees often begin growing in your yard more quickly because they've lost fewer roots in the transplanting process. Keep that in mind when buying.

You can save a lot of money and have a little fun by propagating forsythia, pussy willow, spirea and quince this fall. Take 10- to 12-inch cuttings after the plants have dropped their leaves, dip the cut ends into rooting hormone and plant them eight to nine inches deep in a trench. Keep the trench moist. When the plants bud out in the spring, transplant them into containers. Keep them there for one season unless they look big enough to plant the following fall.

When you're thinking about planting trees this fall, the University of Kentucky recommends avoiding those that are short-lived, have weak branches that make them prone to storm damage, or develop fruit that's more of a nuisance than a treat.

For those reasons, avoid, if possible, box elder, tree of heaven, Lombardy poplar, osage orange, mulberry, silver or water maple, cottonwood, black locust, Siberian elm, European white birch, catalpa and willows.

FRED'S SUPER TIP

With winter banging loudly at the door, let's talk a little bit about chimneys, wood-burning stoves and collecting firewood, a chore millions of Americans are tackling each year.

Improperly maintained chimneys cause 40,000 fires in the United States each year, costing homeowners about $25 million and causing insurance companies to take a much closer look a

wood-heated homes and the applicable insurance rates.

Many of those fires are caused by the creosote deposits found in most chimneys. Chimneys should be inspected every year and professionally cleaned to avoid buildup. If you have a wood-burning stove, it won't hurt to inspect and clean it several times a year during warm winter spells.

But you'll still get a creosote buildup just burning wood in an open fireplace, so here are a few tips to keep your fire burning safely, most of them supplied by safety experts from the University of Kentucky:

Flue temperatures must be more than 250 degrees to reduce creosote formation. If the stovepipe is too long or the chamber inside the chimney too big and not designed for wood-burning stoves, creosote will build up. Too many turns in the pipe will also lead to creosote accumulations.

Many experts are recommending that special insulated stovepipes be run from the wood-burning stove or insert up the inside of the chimney, especially in older houses, to prevent creosote buildup.

These are all factors to be considered before purchasing a wood-burning stove or fireplace insert. To be absolutely sure, check with your local fire department or your insurance agent for proper installation techniques.

Burn dry wood, either pine or hardwood that has been cut, split and stacked for at least six months — a year is better. That's because about half the weight of fresh-cut wood is water, which must be evaporated as steam when the wood starts burning. This costs you heat and causes the cooler smoke to condense on the flue as creosote.

In general, softwoods such as pine, soft maple or sycamore will produce more creosote than hardwoods such as ash, beech, oak, hard maple, hickory and locust, but unseasoned wood is the biggest culprit in creosote buildup.

Be sure to deal with reputable wood salesmen. Know exactly what kind of wood you're buying and how long it has been seasoned. Well-seasoned wood is normally a darker color, and the ends have little splits indicating its dryness.

Avoid prolonged periods of burning with the damper turned way down. Slow-burning fires — and many wood burners will turn their dampers way down at night before going to bed — produce more creosote.

If you insist on that practice, try to compensate by having a hot, vigorous fire for 10 to 15 minutes in the morning to help burn off deposits. It's also smart to start a vigorous fire at night before turning down the damper.

By mixing softwoods with hardwoods you can have an easily ignited but longer-lasting fire. Don't ever burn treated lumber or even lumber scraps you think may have been treated 10 years ago. The preservatives in treated lumber produce very poisonous ashes when burned.

Tests have indicated many of those chemicals sold to put on the fire to prevent creosote buildup are not especially effective and can even produce noxious gases. Use accordingly.

Should a chimney fire occur — and the frightening roar in your chimney will be unmistakable — call the fire department first, and, if possible, cut off the air to the fire by turning down the stove dampers.

Always have a fire extinguisher on hand and be sure there are smoke alarms in every room near the fireplace. A creosote fire can reach 3,000 degrees, and you can't be too careful.

December

⬤⇨ December Checklist

LAWN TIPS

❑ Read the 12-point checklist in this chapter.
❑ Make a New Year's resolution to follow the 12-point checklist after you read it.

EARLY

❑ Prune hollies.
❑ Preserve greens from cedar, boxwood or hollies for Christmas.
❑ Prepare sunny location for Christmas plants.
❑ Prepare amaryllis for blooming.
❑ Continue watering evergreens, weather permitting.
❑ Make sure trees are properly staked to prevent wind damage.
❑ Mulch over mums and foxglove.
❑ Clean up garden and rake lawn.

MIDDLE

❑ Provide humidity for houseplants and clean the leaves of houseplants.
❑ Check to make sure roses and strawberries are properly mulched.
❑ Check stored bulbs and corms for disease.
❑ Keep live Christmas tree well-watered and stored in a cool place.

LATE

❑ Use sand, nitrogen fertilizer or ashes on icy sidewalks and driveways.
❑ Don't use salt.
❑ Toss ashes from fireplace onto the garden.
❑ Continue feeding the birds.
❑ Check houseplants for spider mites.

SUPER TIP

❑ Picking a Christmas tree

December is the month when the seed catalogs arrive, gardeners compile a wish list of presents, and poinsettias and cactuses reign as the holiday flowers. It is, after all, only about 60 days until early planting.

December comes from *decem*, the Latin word for ten. December used to have 29 days, but Julius Caesar added two more.

It's usually warmer in December than during other winter months. The average high temperature in this area in December is 45.4 degrees; the average low 28.9 degrees. The average precipitation — including melted snow — is 3.48 degrees.

The most precipitation ever in Louisville in December was 8.43 inches; the least, .65 inches. The highest-ever temperature was 76 degrees on Dec. 3, 1982. The coldest was minus 9 degrees on Dec. 22, 1960.

The normal snowfall in December is 2.6 inches, but 24.6 inches fell in 1917, including 15 inches in 24 hours, the second heaviest snowstorm in Louisville history.

The most snow in Louisville history was the 50.2 inches that fell in 1917-18, with the winter of 1977-78 right behind it. The most snow ever to fall in Louisville on Christmas Eve was the 8.3 inches that fell in 1939.

There are nine hours and 43 minutes of sun on Dec. 1 and nine hours and 34 minutes on Dec. 31. On Dec. 20, the shortest day of the year, there are nine hours and 31 minutes of sun, and most of it is low in the sky.

The average soil temperature in December is between 41 and 46 degrees.

Walt Disney, who gives many people joy around Christmas, was born Dec. 5, 1901, and Eli Whitney, inventor of the cotton gin, was born on Dec. 8, 1765.

LAWN TIPS

December has never been a good time to think a great deal about the front lawn — except maybe for trying to figure out how to get the snow off its accompanying sidewalk. So maybe what we should do here is take a quick look at a 12-point checklist put together by the National Lawn Institute that will best guarantee that the front yard will look its absolute best six months from now.

You might even make a New Year's resolution to pay full attention to the list, at least until April.

Now here's that 12-point checklist:.

1. Design for use. Lawns are to be used. This means they should be walked on, played on and still be pleasing to look at. Care should be taken in the design of lawns and gardens to provide adequate space for all intended uses.

2. Encourage a mixture of grasses. Use mixtures of grasses — perhaps more than one type of tall fescue — rather than pure seedlings of one cultivar. Mixtures of grasses adjust better to a constantly changing environment than stands consisting of one type. Mixtures

increase the hardiness of your patch.

3. Lawns need sunlight. Don't fight shade. Use groundcovers where there is insufficient light to grow turf. Attempts to grow lawns in shady areas often fail because of the combined effects of low light intensity, root competition from the trees that suck up water and nutrients and poor air movement, which increases disease problems within the turf.

4. Have lawn soils tested. A soil test will indicate the need for lime and will aid in the selection of the right fertilizer for a specific soil. Brand-name fertilizers are recommended for "average" conditions. A soil test will indicate how close your conditions are to average, and if a certain "special" mix right be required.

5. Fertilize in early fall. Fertilize in the early fall — September, October and even into November — every year. Consider fall fertilization a must. That is when grasses store reserves for winter. Don't let your lawn go into dormancy in a starved condition .

6. Feed with nitrogen and potassium. For established lawns use more nitrogen than potassium and phosphorus. A slow-release, high-nitrogen fertilizer is always best. In most cases a lot of phosphorous is needed only while building a new lawn, or if the soil test indicates it's needed.

7. Renovate lawns in the fall. Lawns, like the rest of us, can become "pot-bound," especially bluegrass lawns. If you have a large thatch buildup, or too many weeds, thin out the grass with a de-thatcher, reseed and apply fertilizer when the grass is up and healthy. Grasses need room to grow. Using a newer, tall fescue variety among the older grass will improve its toughness and vigor.

8. Kill non-grassy weeds in the fall. Herbicides aimed at the non-grassy broadleaf weeds — such as plantain and dandelion — are usually most effective in the fall, although frustrated homeowners may also try them in the spring. Ornamental plants most likely to be injured by herbicide drift during the spring and summer are more hardy and less likely to be injured from treatments made after the first frost. Lawn weeds are more easily controlled in the fall by the proper use of the right herbicide.

Mushrooms and fungi of all sorts often show up in the cool, damp weather of spring and fall. There is no effective chemical control because they live off of the decaying organic matter in the soil. Either rake them up, mow them down or get out a golf club and practice tee shots. Above all, don't harvest them. Lots of mushrooms are poisonous.

9. Use pre-emergent herbicides for grassy weeds. Grassy weeds such as crab grass are best handled in early to mid-spring with pre-emergent applications. A post-emergent herbicide should be considered for those weeds that cannot be controlled by a pre-emergent chemical.

10. Mow frequently. The more fre-

quently you mow the more easily the smaller grass clippings will rot into the earth, thus preventing more trips to the local landfill by heavy trucks hauling heavier compost and grass clippings. Remember, today's turf is tomorrow's earth.

11. Water well or don't water at all. Lawns should be watered adequately or they should be left unwatered so that adjustments to drought and dormancy can be made in a natural way. More harm than good often results from sprinklers set to apply less than one-inch of water per setting. Use the type of sprinklers that minimize water runoff.

12. Limit pesticide use. Use fungicides or pesticides only as "special purpose" treatments to control specific disease and insect problems. Use herbicides only when the turf is unable to crowd out weeds on its own. Use pesticides only on lawns that are well cared for; properly mowed, fertilized and watered.

GARDEN TIPS
EARLY

Now is a good time to prune hollies and use their trimmings for indoor decorating. Prune with care, always keeping in mind the natural pyramid shape of a holly tree. If you do a good job of cutting the branches, your tree will already be pruned for the coming season.

Hollies usually need little pruning except to train a leader or to remove dead, diseased and damaged branches. If several stems develop where you want one leader, remove the other stems. If part of a leader is dead or injured, cut it back to healthy wood just above a bud or leaf. If the entire leader is dead, cut it back to the nearest whorl of branches.

You can control the direction a branch grows by pruning it back to the proper bud, which will point in the direction you want the shoot to grow. If you cut a branch back completely to the trunk, or cut a twig back to the branch, new growth may not appear, so cut back only to a bud.

And if you're curious, yes, there are deciduous holly trees available from some nurseries and garden shops. They are especially beautiful in the fall when their brilliant red berries put on an amazing show of color. There is a fine collection of these trees in Bernheim Forest at Clermont, Ky.

If you cut greens such as cedar, boxwood or hollies for Christmas, soak them thoroughly in a tub of water for 24 hours. Then dip the ends in candle wax to seal them. Magnolia leaves can be clipped and dipped in a container of floor wax. It makes them shiny and seals the leaves so they stay shiny longer.

Chances are you'll be getting — and possibly giving — several of the traditional Christmas plants in the next week or so. Here are a few things you should be doing to care for those plants.

They'll need as much natural light as possible, or their leaves will drop like maple leaves in autumn. Prepare a place with lots of bright light but not in the direct sunlight, which will cause leaves to fade.

Maintain a uniform temperature of 65 to 70 degrees, keep the air as humid as possible, maybe with trays filled with pebbles you can water, but keep the plant's soil on the dry side.

The amaryllis, also a common Christmas gift, requires special care. Many arrive in full bloom, but preplanted amaryllis are also easy to grow from bulbs. Water regularly and grow at average room temperatures near a window or under plant lights. The stalks will lengthen daily, and in four to six weeks you'll have huge, lovely blooms.

Or, if you want to save money, pot a bulb yourself and give the amaryllis as a gift. The bulb likes a tight home, so use a pot about an inch larger than the bulb. The pot should have holes in the bottom, which you want to cover with a layer of coarse material, like pebbles, for good drainage. Plant the bulb in commercial potting soil or a mix of loam and peat moss or vermiculite. Plant so the top half of the bulb is above the surface. Firm the soil and water well.

But after that — and this is very important — water sparingly until the flower stem appears. Let the top inch of soil dry well between waterings. As the stem gets longer, increase the water. When it is ready to bloom, apply water-soluble fertilizer.

Oddly enough, the amaryllis often doesn't send up foliage until the flowers begin to open on the stem. If you're lucky and keep the plant in a sunny room with mild temperatures, it will bloom for a month. After the blooms fade, keep the plant in a sunny window as the foliage fades. In the spring, set the plant outside in a partly sunny area, but keep watering and feeding it. By fall the foliage will yellow. Cut off the leaves, let the plant rest for about a month, then begin the cycle again by washing off some of the old dirt with a garden hose. Give it some new soil, a teaspoon of bone meal and begin the process again. Leave the bulb in the pot for three or four years before repotting.

Weather permitting, keep trying to water your evergreen trees because they will lose moisture through their leaves all winter. Deciduous trees don't need that much water — unless they were newly planted — because they don't have leaves. Don't forget to mulch evergreens too.

Check all sizable deciduous plants that went in the ground this fall or last spring, including fruit and ornamental types, to make certain they are properly staked to resist wind damage. Be sure thin-barked trees such as maples are wrapped with burlap, heavy sisal paper or plastic tree wrap Be sure to remove that wrap about April.

Continue to place mulches over valued perennials like mums and foxglove to prevent fluctuating winter temperatures from heaving them from the ground. In a few more weeks the limbs of your discarded Christmas tree will shield the plants but not suffocate them.

I hope you have cleaned up the flower and vegetable garden, pulled up all dead tomato plants and annual flowers and snipped off the blackened top of perennials like peonies all the way down to the ground. Above all, I hope you have raked your lawn so the leaves don't suffocate the grass.

MIDDLE

Check houseplants for brown, dry edges indicating too little humidity in the house. If pebble trays don't work, a humidifier may be a good investment, especially if you plan on increasing your indoor collection. On gloomy days — or weeks — try to move your plants closer to a window. Artificial lighting can help. Reduce watering and withhold fertilizer.

It's also especially important to clean the foliage of your houseplants during the shorter winter days because dust reduces the already diminished light. The easiest way to do this is to set them in the bathtub and squirt them with a fine spray of lukewarm water. Wash your rubby ducky if the mood strikes.

By now you should have protected those precious roses by mounding mulch or dirt over the plants, which should have been cut back to 12 to 14 inches. Strawberries also need a straw mulch by now.

Begin checking your stored canna, gladiolus, dahlia and caladium bulbs and corms to see if any are diseased. Throw out any that look sick. Use a fungicide to protect the rest, although it may be too late.

We've talked several times about preparing a hole in the ground for your living Christmas tree, but now that the time is here you should remember not to keep the tree indoors for more than 10 days because drafts and dryness could kill it. There's also a danger the tree will break dormancy indoors, and putting it outside after that will kill it.

Keep it well-watered indoors. Before planting outdoors let it spend a few days in a cool garage to get readjusted to the cold, cruel world. When planting, water well, stake and mulch.

LATE

As tempting as it is, avoid using salt on sidewalks and driveways, especially near trees and shrubs. Salt injures trees and shrubs. Try sand, nitrogen fertilizer, ashes or better yet, potassium chloride. It will melt ice at temperatures down to 40 degrees below zero and will not damage plants.

In any case, all remaining ice-melting materials should be removed as soon as the ice is gone.

Speaking of ashes, now is the perfect time to toss all the ashes from your holiday fires onto your garden. In general, good-quality, unleached ashes will contain about 5 to 10 percent potash, 1 to 2 percent phosphate and 50 to 70 percent limestone equivalent.

So while there is some benefit in adding wood ashes, you should remember they contain no nitrogen, the most important fertilizing element. But when wood ash is applied at the rate of 40 to 50 pounds per 1,000 square feet — which is easily obtained from a winter of burning wood — it will supply enough potash for most lawns and gardens.

Also, because of its high lime content, ashes should never be dumped around acid-loving plants like azaleas and rhododendrons.

If you've already started feeding birds for the winter, keep it up. While you're at it, an electrically heated bird bath can be a real focal point for birds, your feeder and you.

Keep a sharp eye out for spider-mite invasions of your plants. They love warm, dry air, and regular spraying may be needed to keep your plants safe.

This is perhaps the best chore of the year. Pick a quiet moment, walk around your house or yard, and count your blessings. We all get so busy during the holidays trying to get all the "family" things done that we often forget what a blessing it is to have our families with us.

There's nothing more important than family, and what better time to enjoy it.

FRED'S TIPS

If you are making a list, checking it twice, trying to find out who's naughty or nice, and you've got a nice gardener on your list, I've got some suggestions for you.

A good gardener can always use

tools, like a hand pruner or digging tools. It may cost a little more, but look for sturdiness, durability and balance. I received a set of hand tools a few Christmases back made of solid pieces of aluminum. They are easy to clean and have a "pistol grip" so they do not slip from my grasp.

Consider a "soaker hose," which is the most efficient way to water. The hose has holes punched in it every few inches, allowing the water to drip out directly into the soil instead of gushing out the end.

Hose-attached sprayers are also useful. One of the best I have ever used is called a "hose sprayer with a metering dial." It has a dial that allows you to attach a bottle to the bottom and monitor exactly how much chemical you use.

Also give houseplants, bulbs that can be forced indoors and even packs of seeds as stocking stuffers. If you want to give live plants, traditional ones such as poinsettia, Christmas cactus, cyclamen, ornamental pepper, Jerusalem cherry and begonia are good. It's an excellent way to say, "Happy holidays, and here's wishing you the happiest of gardening years."

And hey, don't forget this: What could be a better present than a copy of "The New Fred Wiche Lawn & Garden Almanac"?

Chestnuts are very good eating at Christmas, if you can get to the meat of the matter. To do it, poke a hole in the flat side of the shell, place a bunch in a kitchen pot and cover with boiling water for 15 to 20 minutes. Take out a few at a time to eat; it's easier to get to the meat when they're hot.

For roasting, put them in a heavy skillet in three tablespoons of cooking oil per pound of nuts. Bring them to a sizzle, then stick them in the oven for 20 minutes at 400 degrees.

Ummmmmmmmm, good.

The rabbit's-foot fern is a good choice for a winter gift because it tolerates dry air better than many other ferns. Give it bright, indirect light and keep it away from drafts. Keep the soil moist but not soggy. Mist once a week and feed it 20-20-20 fertilizer at half the recommended rate.

Don't leave your insecticides and fungicides outside in the garage or storage shed in cold weather. The ideal storage temperature is 60 degrees or higher. Don't ever let the temperature drop below 40 degrees, which could destroy the chemical combinations and render the spray ineffective.

The following, ranked in order from the most heat-efficient to the least heat-efficient, is a list of commonly available firewood in this area. They are shagbark hickory, black locust, hard maple, apple, white oak, white ash, black walnut, black ash, soft maple and poplar. Be sure you know what you're buying. Gas-station attendants often don't.

If we happen to have a very heavy snowfall, you might go out and trample down the snow around the trunks of your very young fruit trees. It will discourage rodents from moving in to eat; packed snow is hard to bore through.

Bird feeders are great, but you can help birds get through the winter and improve your landscape at the same time by planting shrubs and trees that grow food birds like to eat, as well as providing protection near the feeder. So make a note, and next spring plant some winterberry, scarlet firethorn, chokeberry, sumac, burning bush, crab apple, cotoneaster and viburnum to grow bird food.

Sometimes people have a difficult time keeping their cyclamen healthy and in bloom. Just be sure the soil never becomes dry enough to cause even slight wilting of the plant and flowers. It also does best in half-sunny windows, where there are no drafts and temperatures from 50 to 70 degrees.

If you're buying an indoor plant in this weather, ask the salesperson to wrap it in floral wrapping to protect it from the cold and chill. Preheat your car to prevent chill injury. Never leave it in an unattended car while shopping. Make the nursery your last stop before heading home.

I keep an old bucket of oily sand in my tool shed to use in cleaning my tools. Every time I change oil in a piece of lawn or gardening equipment I pour the oil in the sand. The abrasive action does a wonderful job of cleaning off the dirt, and the oil provides protection against rust.

If your fuchsia plant made it through the summer, it needs to be "winterized." Cut the stems back to eight inches in length, keep the growing medium quite dry through the winter, give it some light and keep the temperature cool but not freezing. Next spring resume watering and feeding.

To prevent stored fertilizer from absorbing moisture and turning into "Christmas cake," place it in a sealed plastic bag or waterproof container with a snug-fitting lid. Store in a dry location.

FRED'S SUPER TIP

Every year about now an uncommon sight presents itself on the wind-swept, forested hillsides of Kentuckiana. Hundreds of city folk, spurred by the romance of cutting down a yule tree, descend upon tree farms to play Paul Bunyan.

The idea is that you drive into the country to saw down a Christmas tree. It should be fun rather than frustrating. So here is some advice:

1. It is always a good idea to telephone the tree farm ahead of time to make sure of the supply — especially if you wait until Christmas Eve.

2. A thermos filled with hot chocolate or coffee can help ease the sting of a biting wind.

3. Bring cash. Farms don't have machines that accept credit cards. And checks may be frowned upon.

4. Wear warm clothes. This isn't as obvious as it sounds. City folk are often surprised by the chill out on the back 40. Don't wear your Sunday-go-to-meetin' shoes, especially if there's been a lot of rain. It's going to be muddy, so wear shoes with good traction.

5. Bring a saw if you can. Loaners generally are available but expect a waiting line for one. Hatchets and axes are not recommended. They are inferior to saws in cutting trees and are like a time bomb for the accident-prone.

6. Then there is twine. You will need some to bind the tree to the car. (Don't forget: stump end toward the front bumper. Reverse it and even at 55 mph you will be decorating the highway with pine branches all the way home.) And if you're driving one of those little compact cars, don't expect to bring home a giant of the woods. You are liable to scare someone to death when

they see this big tree coming at them in the rear-view mirror.

7. And finally, remember that trees always look smaller when you see them in the great outdoors. So before starting out measure the space in the room that the tree will occupy. There's no point in going out and cutting a 14-foot tree if you are going to have to lop four feet off the bottom when you get it home.

If you intend to buy your tree from a corner lot, here are some guidelines to follow in making your selection.

1. Be sure the tree has needles that are relatively pliant and firmly attached to the twigs. If the needles are brittle and tend to snap or shatter when bent between your fingers, the tree may be dry or frozen, depending on weather conditions.

2. When you get the tree home, cut off 1 or 1 1/2 inches from the butt and promptly stand the tree in a pail of fresh warm water. The amount of water consumed can vary considerably, depending on the species, condition and size of the tree and on the temperatures and relative humidity of the room.
If the tree is six to seven feet tall and if room temperature and humidity are average for early December, you might discover that a good tree can take up a pint of water during a 24-hour period.

3. Keep water in the Christmas-tree stand at all times. A big tree may use

two quarts of water during the first 24 hours it is inside and may average a quart or more a day for the first week. A freshly cut tree may take up considerably less water.

4. For several years I have doused our Christmas tree with an anti-dessicant spray called "Wilt-Proof" before bringing it inside. This material seals the needles, prevents moisture from being lost, and keeps the tree fresher longer. It seems to have helped a lot, but always remember: There is no such thing as a fireproof Christmas tree.

I'd like to take this time to thank you for reading this book, and to wish each and every one of you a Merry Christmas and a Happy New Year.

Organic
Gardening

A lot of people believe organic gardening is a great concept, but what in the world do you do when bugs and diseases show up?

To be honest, there are still a few vegetables and fruits that are almost impossible to raise without resorting to some sort of insecticide or fungicide, even the supposedly "safer" biological ones.

But we've learned that it's totally wrong to douse your bean patch with 300 gallons of Insta-Death at the first sighting of a Japanese beetle.

We've done far too much of that over the years.

There are a lot of organic practices you can follow to eliminate chemicals from your garden. It will take a little more diligence and work, but it will also bring you a lot closer to Mother Nature, who never did like chemicals in her kitchen anyway.

To be organic you will have to accept the notion that the insects are going to get some of your plants, or at least a few of the leaves. Be ready to plant a little extra – some for the bugs and a lot for you – and everyone's karma will improve.

Meanwhile, here are a few things to think about to improve your bargaining position. They come under the gardening buzz words of the 1990s: Integrated Pest Management, or IMP.

1. Know your enemy. Random and poorly timed spraying not only kills marauding bugs and caterpillars, it also kills the bees that pollinate flowers, the ladybugs that eat aphids and the praying mantises that eat all kinds of bugs.

2. Organic gardening requires almost daily hand-to-hand combat. You'll have to get down on your hands and knees there in the cabbage patch and look for the slugs, caterpillars, worms and beetles. The best time to hunt is in the morning when the bugs are least active, although you may have a tough time explaining why you're late to the boss.

Then comes the real hard part: You've got to be willing to pick the bugs off. Just drop them in a plastic bottle you can slap a lid on later. Some people drop them in a small jar of motor oil and 10-W-30 them to death. Or just use a container of water with a thin layer of kerosene or oil.

Actually, picking off all your Japanese beetles may require a 55-gallon drum. But they're so dumb they mostly drop straight down after being disturbed and are fairly easy to catch.

Also, be on the alert for the homes of various bagworms and tent caterpillars that will build baggy houses in your trees. Cut them off in early evening while the insects are in the houses and burn them.

3. Use dormant-oil sprays. This is an important and easy method for stopping scale, spider mites and leaf rollers on fruit trees and ornamentals. Dormant-oil sprays should be used in early spring, but be sure the temperature is above freezing. The sprays are non-toxic. They "suffocate" the pests trapped beneath the oil but do not harm the trees.

4. You can also beat a lot of bugs

before they get started. The dreaded Colorado potato beetle, for instance, lays its eggs in orange clusters beneath plant leaves. Squish them between your thumb and forefinger and you'll have a great start in keeping them out of your spuds. If they get to adult size, they're easily picked off plants.

5. A simple as it sounds, sometimes a steady blast with a water hose will keep bugs off your plants. The more persistent ones will try to jump right back in the saddle, but daily dousings could send them packing. Just don't blow down all your bean plants in the process.

6. Simple barriers can eliminate some bugs. Placing lightweight cardboard collars or paper cups around the base of plants such as cabbage, lettuce and tomatoes will keep the cutworm frustrated and hungry. Be sure to place the collars so that they stick into the ground about an inch deep and extend a few inches above the ground. Aluminum foil can help discourage striped cucumber beetles, mites and squash bugs.

7. One increasingly popular method to keep bugs at bay is to cover your crops with the mesh barriers now on the market. The screens may be a little expensive, but they can last for years. They'll allow much of the sun and all of the rain to get through but will keep the insects waiting in the lobby.

Be sure to spread the mesh tightly and seal the edges. But don't nail it down too tightly; you'll have to remove the barrier to weed and to allow insects inside to pollinate when the plants have set flowers. You can also make or buy "cone screens" for individual cabbage or head-lettuce plants.

8. As yucky as it sounds, some gardeners collect insects in a jar, mix them up with water in an old blender and spray the concoction back onto the plants as a not-so-subtle warning to other bugs.

9. Rotate your crops every year, even in the smallest gardens. It may seem silly, but some bugs don't like to travel much, and moving the plants around helps confuse them.

10. Be more aware of plant cycles. Cabbage, for instance, is less likely to be attacked by the root maggot if it is planted late. In fact, I generally have much less of an insect problem with my fall gardens than I do with those planted early. I guess the bugs are worn out by autumn.

11. Look hard to find disease-resistant plants, shrubs and trees, especially ornamentals. With organic gardening becoming more popular, the plant and seed companies are working overtime to develop varieties that are especially resistant to diseases. They are proud of their new varieties and make a point of bragging about them in their catalogs. If you have a plant that is already lost to disease, however, pull it up and throw it away. Far away.

12. You can use insect traps in your gardens. However, in the case of Japanese beetles, my research has shown that the traps might actually draw more beetles to your yard than the traps can handle. So the traps can be counterproductive.

For slugs, sink a shallow container of beer to the rim in the dirt. The slugs are drawn to the beer, crawl in and expire in a beery death.

You might consider laying old boards in your garden rows. Night-feeding bugs might try to hide under them; one quick lift and you can dispatch them with your boots.

Whiteflies are easily lured to a piece of wood painted bright yellow and smeared with oil or molasses. Apple maggots, on the other hand, are attracted to bright red croquet balls smeared with a sticky substance.

13. Try not to work in the garden when it is wet. As you move around you compact the earth and may be hauling diseases along with you.

14. When all is said and stomped, the one best way to keep your plants healthy is to keep your garden healthy. If your soil is not rich and well-drained, keep adding compost, leaves or manure. Be certain to water deeply and at the right times.

15. Use a lot of trellises, cages and stakes to keep plants off the ground and improve air circulation. Use clean mulch, but not too thickly because it can also provide a home for pests. About four inches of mulch is plenty.

16. Pay a lot of attention to garden maintenance. Plow deeply, clean up the garden in the fall and throw away rotted food. Don't leave it around for the bugs to use as a summer condo. Keep your garden weed-free all year, and mow neatly around its edges if possible. Keep your tools clean, if not disinfected.

ORGANIC INSECTICIDES AND SPRAYS

All right, you tried squishing bug eggs, picking bugs off by hand and putting up protective barriers, and a few pests still got through. You think the problem is so serious you need to use some sprays from naturally occurring substances or insecticidal soap.

They can work, but remember: Even "organic" insecticides can't tell bug pests from bug pals, and you run the risk of killing all of them.

Here's a quick list of what's available.

1. You can buy an expensive substance called diatomaceous earth, which is the ground-up remains of marine organisms. The earth is spread on the plants. It contains sharp-edged silica that cuts into the bodies of the insects both internally and externally, ending their feeding habits. But it won't hurt you.

2. Sprays of bacillus thuringensis, which is a naturally occurring bacterium, will spread diseases to many caterpillars and borers. It's often sold under the name Dipel or Thuricide. It's spread on plants, the bugs eat it, become paralyzed and drop off into oblivion.

Milky spore disease, which doesn't sound like much fun, in another bacterium that will help eliminate Japanese beetles, although it, as well as bacillus thuringensis, can be expensive.

3. Pyrethrum, which is made from the ground-up flowers of mums, is a botanical insecticide that kills on contact. It eliminates aphids, caterpillars

and beetles. It is derived from plants and breaks down soon after being used, but it is still a potent pesticide and should be used with caution. It needs to be sprayed directly on the insects.

4. Rotenone is a powerful, slow-acting, plant-derived insecticide made from the ground-up roots of tropical plants, including derris and timbo. It is not harmful to warm-blooded animals but is lethal to fish, so don't use it near your farm pond. Rotenone breaks down in the sunlight and loses its power in a week.

5. Insecticidal soaps. These are sold commercially and are much gentler than tossing two cups of Tide into a bucket and going to work. In fact, cleaning plants with home-made remedies could even "burn" them. Be sure to use insecticidal soaps according to their directions. They help control soft-bodied insects such as aphids, spider mites and whiteflies. They must be applied several times a week to be effective.

6. One new development is a pesticide called Margosan-O, which was developed from the Neem tree in India. Margosan-O, which comes from two compounds of the tree, has been registered for use against whiteflies, mites and caterpillars and has shown to be helpful in fighting fungus growth.

It has been marketed on a test basis in Florida and is still being tested by the U.S. Department of Agriculture to determine how long it is effective after being sprayed.

ORGANIC FERTILIZERS

Not only is compost a great soil conditioner, it can also do wonders as a general-purpose fertilizer. I've always used chemical fertilizers with good results, but there are also many organic fertilizers that can be used with good result, although they may be a little more expensive and harder to find.

It's best, of course, to develop the soil slowly with annual applications of organic mixes such as composted cow manure. With a big garden it will take a lot of work, but you should find it rewarding.

Here's a brief list of some organic fertilizers and their uses.

BONE MEAL – This is an excellent source of phosphorus, which is especially good for bulbs and flower beds. It is sold as raw bone meal and steamed bone meal.

FISH EMULSION – It can be applied as a foliar spray early in the morning or in the evening. It is a good general-purpose fertilizer, especially in the spring.

COMPOSTED COW MANURE – It can be used 40 to 50 pounds per 100 square feet. It is a slow-release fertilizer, so it actually helps condition the soil more than it boosts the plants' growth.

COTTONSEED MEAL – This produce acidifies the soil so it can be used around acid-loving plants such as azaleas and blueberries. It will last four to six months.

GREENSAND – This is good for loosening clay soils. It can last for many years and contains many trace minerals.

WOOD ASHES – Put these on the

soil in the spring and dig them in. They have many trace elements but should not be used near plants such as azaleas or rhododendrons.

MAKING COMPOST

Gardeners can create a treasure of rich organic material by using general yard trash and kitchen wastes in a compost pile. Compost is organic, and making compost is good for the environment. There are a number of commercially produced composting bins. These are available through garden centers and catalogs, but you can make compost in your own backyard.

Grass clippings, leaves, branches cut into small pieces and general garden trash make a good compost pile. Kitchen wastes that do not contain fats can also be used. Good choices include carrot and potato peelings, ends of asparagus spears, apple, lettuce and cabbage cores, pepper stems and cores, melon rinds and onion, orange and banana peels.

Compost improves soil texture, especially in heavy clay soils. This reduces erosion and maximizes the benefits of water. In addition, more oxygen can penetrate the soil. Composting also recycles nutrients into the soil, cutting down on the need and expense of using synthetic fertilizers.

Ample moisture and oxygen are the secret to making good compost. Water your compost pile periodically if the weather is dry. Turn the compost over every three to six weeks as this improves the oxygen flow.

Most compost piles measure 4 feet by 4 feet or 4 feet by 8 feet. Piles that are over 4 feet high decrease oxygen movement. If there is an odor problem, add a cup of lime per square foot of compost.

INDOOR GARDENING

Houses, apartments, offices, school rooms — almost any place is a good place for growing plants inside. Indoor gardens are nice because they don't depend on the seasons or the weather. I like indoor gardens because they make you feel good.

Plants respond to you in ways that cats and dogs do not — and you don't have to walk your plants! Plants add color and beauty to all kinds of spaces, and you are limited only by the amount of space you have for growing.

To begin, you will need a few simple tools and supplies. As your garden expands, you may want to add others.

Supplies should be available at garden centers, supermarkets or variety stores.

You will need a variety of pots and containers, drainage material such as pebbles or gravel, potting soil, plant food, a water can, a small trowel and some plants!

WHAT AND WHERE TO PLANT

Indoor plants can be grown in flowerpots, flat dishes, window boxes, big bottles, hanging baskets and many other containers. Your containers should suit the plants you choose. In window boxes use plants of various heights. Place taller plants in the center and use smaller plants around the sides.

For individual plants, you will want the size of your container to fit the size of your plant.

Plants for indoor gardens may be purchased from garden centers, catalogs and some supermarkets. You can learn how to take slips or cuttings from other gardeners' plants in the September chapter of this book.

Indoor plants tend to fall into five categories. Here are some of the easiest varieties to grow.

- Flowering plants — African violet
- Green foliage plants — Chinese evergreen.
- Colored foliage plants — Coleus
- Vines or trailing plants — Philodendron
- Desert plants — Peperomia

As you select plant varieties a lot of consideration must be given to the amount of light they need. Plants will fall into three basic "light" categories.

Sunlight: Areas that receive five or more hours of sunlight.

Moderate light: Areas that receive approximately two hours of light, usually in the morning or afternoon.

Shade or semi-shade: Areas in the center of rooms, or windows with a northern exposure.

Most plants grow best in even temperatures. If you have plants in a window, remove them when the weather becomes extremely hot or cold. Avoid putting your plants in drafty places and do not set them on television sets, registers or other places that generate heat and cold.

HOW TO PLANT

The way you plant is just as important as what you plant. Remember, always use a clean container with a drainage hole at the bottom.

Step 1: Put one inch of drainage material (pebbles or gravel) in the bottom of your container. The container should be one size large than the original.

Step 2: Fill half the container with potting soil mixture. Smooth the soil.

Step 3: Remove the plant from its original container and check the root ball. Use your fingers to carefully loosen the root system.

Step 4: Center your plant in the container and add more soil around the edges.

Step 5: Press the soil firmly around the plant.

Step 6: Use remaining soil to fill the container to within 1/2 inch of the top edge. Smooth the soil once again.

PLANT CARE

You already know that plants need the right amount of food, water, light and air. Feed and water your plants when they need it! Don't fall into the trap of feeding and watering on a strict schedule. You'll end up killing your plants.

FEEDING

The easiest way to feed your plants is to purchase commercially developed plant food and read the directions for its use. I think water-soluble types of food are the best and easiest to use. There are several organic plant foods available, but don't be surprised if they are more expensive than traditional foods.

Flowering plants need plant food that is high in phosphorus, and they should be fed no more than twice a month. Foliage plants need food that is high in nitrogen and may be fed once a month from April through September.

All plants need a rest. As the amount and intensity of sunlight diminishes during the winter, plant growth will slow down. Cut back on both food and water during this time.

WATERING

More plants die from overwatering than for any other reason. There is no specific rule about how often to water your plants. The amount of water needed depends on many things such as the size and type of container, the amount of humidity and sunlight in the room as well as the type of plant.

My rule of thumb for watering is to feel the soil in the top of the pot. If it is dry about one inch down, then water thoroughly. I cannot stress this enough. Add water until it seeps out the drainage hole.

Always water from the top. Even if your Great-Aunt Sarah watered her African violets from the bottom — DON'T. Watering from the top flushes out the soil. To water properly, fill the space between the soil and the rim of the container with water and let it soak in. Repeat the process until the soil stops absorbing water.

Collected rainwater or melted snow is excellent for your plants. If you use tap water, fill a separate container and let it sit for 24 hours before using it on your plants. This allows the chemicals to evaporate. Always use tepid water — never hot or cold. To help prevent root rot, never let plants sit in water. Be especially carefully when using pots with saucers attached.

Many plants enjoy and need humidity. There are several ways to increase humidity. One way is to group plants together. This arrangement will generate more humidity.

Another method is to set plants on large, deep saucers that are filled with gravel. Add water. The plants will be sitting on the gravel rather than in the water. As the water evaporates, the humidity increases. And if you are an avid indoor gardener, buy a room humidifier. It's better for you, better for your furniture and better for your plants.

Misting your plants does little good and it can cause the spread of foliage disease.

GROOMING

Your plants will look better and stay healthier if you groom them regularly.

• Pick off dead leaves and flowers. This eliminates places for insects to hide.

• Shape your plants by pinching off new shoots as necessary.

• For plants with large leaves, carefully sponge off dust with warm water or put them in the shower.

• Plants tend to grow toward light. Turn your plants occasionally to keep them from becoming lopsided.

• DO NOT polish your plants with milk or mayonnaise. This closes pores and can kill your plants.

REPOTTING

As your plants get bigger, they will need bigger containers. One sign that you need to repot is when you see roots peeking out of the drainage hole. When repotting, increase the size of your containers one size only. Never go from a very small pot to a very large pot in one step.

To repot, turn the plant upside down with the stem between your fingers. Tap the bottom of the container and the whole plant should drop out.

Loosen the soil around the roots and plant in a larger container following the same steps for when you first potted your plant.

VACATION TIME

When it's time to head off on vacation, don't forget your plants. If you plan to be gone for two weeks or less, there are a couple of ways to ensure your plants' survival. If you will be away for several weeks, you may have to consider a house sitter — or at the very least a friend who will water but not drown your houseplants.

1. Place bricks in the bottom of your bathtub. Fill the tub with water stopping just below the top level of the bricks. Set your plants on the bricks and cover your tub with clear plastic. This creates a greenhouse effect, but you must be sure that the tub does not receive any direct sunlight.

2. The very last thing you should do before leaving on your trip is to water your plants thoroughly and let them drain. Take dark plastic garbage bags and put a pot in each bag. The bag should cover the pots only — not the plants. Carefully tie the top of the bag around the stem and move all plants to the coolest place in the house, away from any windows.

3. If you are traveling in the spring or summer, you may choose to put your indoor plants outside. Select a shady spot in your garden and completely bury the pots in the soil. Water thoroughly.

MOVING

Plants must be moved as carefully as your antique furniture. Contact your moving company and ask them to furnish you with boxes that have cardboard dividers in the bottoms. Some companies may even have specially prepared boxes for moving plants.

Line the inside of the packing boxes with wet newspapers. Water your plants just before putting them on the truck. Remember: Your plants should be the last things on the truck and the first things off.

If you are moving out of state, check on agricultural restrictions in your new state. Some plants may not be allowed across the borders or they may have to go through quarantine.

ORGANIC GARDENING TIPS

As with outdoor gardening, houseplants can do very well without being coated with layers of petroleum-based insecticides and pesticides, provided you are willing to spend a little extra time keeping them safe and happy.

We have already discussed the fact that different plants have different light, water and food requirements, but that needs to be stressed again. A happy plant is a healthy plant.

Here are a few things you can do to ensure happy, healthy plants.

1. Wash your plants occasionally. Give them a shower or hold them upside down over the sink and let the tap water wash over them if they are small enough. Do what you can to keep them clean.

2. One "organic" insecticide used on houseplants is pyrethrum. It's made of ground-up flowers of mums and will work against aphids and beetles. It quickly breaks down but is potent and should be used carefully.

3. Small infestations of aphids can be squashed with your fingers. Whiteflies can be captured by painting a board bright yellow and coating it with oil or a sticky substance. Whiteflies love yellow — sometimes to death.

4. Inspect all plants carefully before buying them. Look for signs of insects or diseases. Don't bring home trouble. Many bugs and diseases hitchhike into the house.

5. If you see a problem with your houseplant, act quickly. There's not always time for a second opinion. Move the plant to a better location, give it a good cleaning, pick off diseased areas, do what it takes to help the plant. If it is totally infested with bugs or some sort of rot, the best answer may be to throw it out.

6. If you're using organic sprays, be sure to cover nearby fish tanks or bird cages; a drifting mist can cause problems.

7. With quick-moving insects such as whiteflies or aphids, spray the neighboring plants too; those rascals change addresses pretty quickly. Slow-footed pests like scale or mealybugs are less likely to spread quickly.

8. Scale can be found along the main vein, under leaves and on stems of plants. About the size of the head of a pin, scale is usually tan, brown or black in color. A cotton swab soaked in rubbing alcohol will get rid of it.

9. Let me re-emphasize to obey watering rules religiously. You may be the biggest reason your plant is rotting or wilting.

TIMES FOR SIDEDRESSING VEGETABLES

Crop	Time of Application
Asparagus	Before growth starts in spring.
Beans	After heavy blossom and set of pods.
Beets	Additional nitrogen might reduce yield or lower quality.
Broccoli	3 weeks after transplanting.
Cabbage	3 weeks after transplanting.
Cauliflower	3 weeks after transplanting.
Carrots	Additional nitrogen might reduce yield or lower quality.
Cucumbers	Apply 1 week after blossoming begins and same amount 3 weeks later.
Eggplant	After first fruit set.
Kale	When plants are about one-third grown.
Lettuce	Additional nitrogen might reduce yield or lower quality.
Muskmelons	Apply 1 week after blossoming begins and same amount 3 weeks later.
Onions	1 to 2 weeks after bulb formation starts.
Parsnips	Additional nitrogen might reduce yield or lower quality.
Peas	After heavy bloom and set of pods.
Peppers	After first fruit set.
Potatoes	After tuber formation starts (bloom stage), about 6 weeks after planting.
Spinach	When plants are about one-third grown.
Squash	Additional nitrogen might reduce yield or lower quality.
Sweet corn	When plants are 12 inches tall.
Sweet potatoes	Additional nitrogen might reduce yield or lower quality.
Tomatoes	Apply 1 to 2 weeks before first picking and same amount 2 weeks after first picking.
Turnips	Additional nitrogen might reduce yield or lower quality.
Watermelon	Additional nitrogen might reduce yield or lower quality.

Source: University of Kentucky, College of Agriculture

VEGETABLE PLANTING GUIDE

Crop	Number of Transplants or Seeds Per Foot	Distance Between Plants When Thinned or Transplanted (inches)	Distance Between Rows (inches)	Planting Depth (inches)
Asparagus	1 crown	18	30	6-8
Beans, bush, lima	6-8 seeds	3-4	30	1-2
Beans, bush, snap	8 seeds	2-3	30	1-2
Beets	10 seeds	4	12-18	½-1
Broccoli	1 transplant	18	30	
Brussels sprouts	1 transplant per 2 ft.	18-24	36	
Cabbage	1 transplant	12-18	30	
Carrots	15-20 seeds	2-3	12-18	½
Cauliflower	1 transplant	18	30	
Cucumbers	3-4 seeds	6-12	30-48	½-1
Kale	4-6 seeds	8-12	18-30	½
Kohlrabi	6-8 seeds	3-6	18-30	½
Lettuce, head	1 transplant	12-15	18-24	½
Lettuce, leaf	10-20 seeds	1-2	12-18	½
Muskmelons	2-3 seeds or 1 transplant	24	30-48	½-1
Okra	3 seeds	12-15	30	1
Onions, from seed	10-15 seeds	2-4	12-18	½-1
Onions	3-6 transplants or sets	2-4	12-18	2-3
Parsley	10-15 seeds	4-6	12-18	½
Parsnips	15-20 seeds	3-4	18-30	½-1
Peas	10-12 seeds	Do not thin	30	2
Peppers	1 transplant	18	30	
Potatoes	1 seed piece	10-12	30	4
Pumpkins	1-2 seeds	10-12 ft.	72	1
Radishes, spring	10-15 seeds	1	12-18	½
Rhubarb	1 crown per 2 ft.	24	30	
Spinach	12-15 seeds	2-4	12-30	½
Squash, summer	2-3 seeds in hill	24	30	
Sweet corn	2-3 seeds	9-12, single plants	30	1-2
Sweet potatoes	1 slip	12-18	30	
Tomatoes	1 transplant per 2 ft.	18-24	30	
Watermelons	1-2 seeds in row	6-8 ft.	72	1

Source: University of Kentucky, College of Agriculture

CRITICAL TIMES TO WATER VEGETABLES

Vegetable	Critical period of water needs
Asparagus	Fern growth
Bean, lima	Pollination and pod development
Bean, snap	Pod enlargement
Broccoli	Establishment, head development
Cabbage	Establishment, head development
Carrot	Establishment, root enlargement
Cauliflower	Establishment, head development
Corn, sweet	Silking, tasseling and ear development
Cucumber	Flowering and fruit development
Eggplant	Uniform supply from flowering through harvest
Melon	Fruit set and early development
Onion, dry	Bulb enlargement
Pea	Flowering and seed enlargement
Pepper	Uniform supply from flowering through harvest
Potato	Tuber set and tuber enlargement
Radish	Root enlargement
Squash, summer	Bud development, flowering and fruit development
Tomato	Uniform supply from flowering through harvest
Turnip	Root enlargement

BULB PLANTING GUIDE

Flowering Time	Planting Depth (inches)	Spacing (inches)	Flowering Height (inches)
Early Spring			
Snowdrops	5	3	Up to 6
Winter Aconite	5	3	Up to 6
Iris Reticulata	5	3	Up to 6
Crocus	5	3	Up to 6
Anemone Blanda	5	3	Up to 6
Kaufmanniana Tulip	8	6	Up to 6
Fosteriana Tulip	8	6	6 to 12
Single Early Tulip	8	6	6 to 12
Double Early Tulip	8	6	6 to 12
Miniature Daffodil	8	4	6 to 12
Hyacinths	8	6	6 to 12
Trumpet Daffodil	8	6	12 to 20
Mid-Spring			
Triumph Tulip	8	5	12 to 20
Daffodils	8	6	12 to 20
Darwin Hybrid Tu- lip	8	6	20 to 28
Greigii Tulip	8	6	6 to 20
Fritillaria Imperialis	8	12	Over 28
Late Spring			
Parrot Tulip	8	6	12 to 20
Double Late Tulip	8	6	12 to 20
Lily-Flowered Tulip	8	6	20 to 28
Darwin Tulip	8	6	20 to 28
Cottage Tulip	8	6	20 to 28
Rembrandt Tulip	8	6	20 to 28
Spanish Bluebells	5	6	6 to 12
Dutch Iris	8	4	12 to 20
Allium Giganteum	8	8	Over 28

CROP TIMETABLE

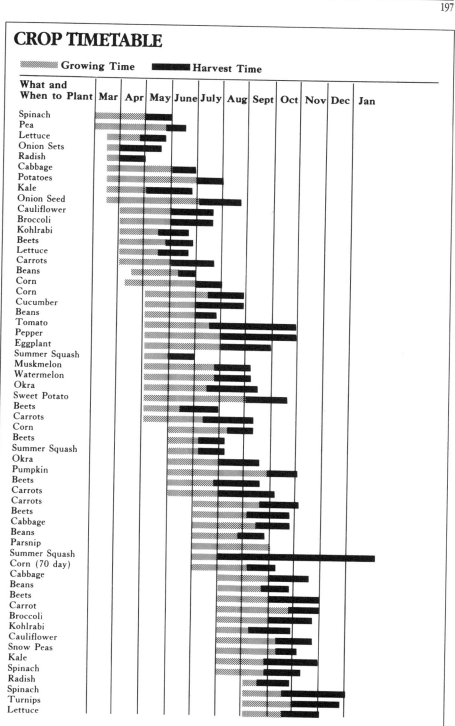

COMMON GARDEN INSECTS

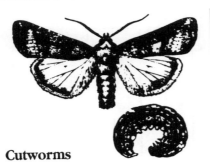

Cutworms

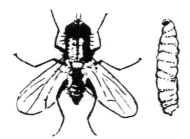

Root Maggots

Imported Cabbageworm

Mites

Colorado Potato Beetle

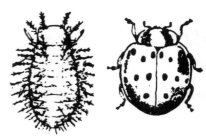

Mexican Bean Beetle

Cucumber Beetle

Corn Earworm

Squash Vine Borers

Leafhoppers

Japanese Beetle

Wireworms

Cabbage Looper

Stalk Borer

Hornworm

Flea Beetle

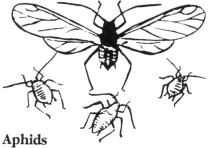

Aphids

COLD TEMPERATURE TOLERANCE OF VEGETABLES

Tender (damaged by light frost)	**Semi-Hardy** (tolerate light frost)	**Hardy** (tolerate hard frost)
Beans	Beets	Broccoli
Cucumber	Carrot	Brussels sprouts
Eggplants	Cauliflower	Cabbage
Muskmelon	Celery	Collards
New Zealand spinach	Chard	Kale
Okra	Chinese cabbage	Kohlrabi
Pepper	Endive	Mustard greens
Pumpkin	Lettuce	Onion
Squash	Parsnip	Parsley
Sweet Corn	Potato	Peas
Sweet Potato	Salsify	Radish
Tomato		Spinach
Watermelon		Turnip

Index

N

O